D1384049

DOG ON A LOG™
Pup Books
Book 2

I am not a Reading Specialist or certified educator, but I do have a lot of experience teaching my daughter with dyslexia how to read. At times, it was difficult to determine what to do and how to do it. It is my hope that the information provided within this book will make the journey a bit easier for other parents. The content provided herein is for informational purposes and does not take the place of an evaluation and teaching plan provided by a credentialed educator. Every effort has been made to ensure that the content provided here is accurate and helpful for my readers. However, this is not an exhaustive treatment of the subject. No liability is assumed for losses or damages due to the information provided. You should consult a credentialed educator for specific guidance on educating your child, yourself, or others.

DOG ON A LOG Books
Tucson, Arizona

Public Domain images from www.clker.com

Traceable block letters (except lowercase 'b') by
Print Designs by Kris

Traceable D'Nealian font and lines (except lowercase "b" with arrows or stars) created by DN KidLetter.
http://guindo.pntic.mec.es/jmag0042/kidfonts.html
Stars and internal arrows added by Pamela Brookes.

ISBN: 978-1648310089

Library of Congress Control Number:2019906177

www.dogonalogbooks.com

THE
SQUIGGLE CODE
(LETTERS MAKE WORDS)

DOG ON A LOG Pup Books
Book 2

By Pamela Brookes
Edited by Nancy Mather Ph.D.

Sight Words Introduced in "The Squiggle Code"

Letter Group 1: the, is

Letter Group 2: a, and, to, has

Letter Group 4: does, go, of

Letter Group 5: her, says

From
Before the Squiggle Code

Spoken language is a code. The code starts with random sounds that we group together into words. Then we put several words together to make sentences. By talking and by listening to each other's words and sentences, we share ideas with other human beings.

Reading and writing are another type of code for sharing ideas. This code involves squiggles. We happen to call those squiggles letters.

We put squiggles on a piece of paper and tell a child, "Tell me what this says."

Yet those squiggles are silent. They do not make any noise. Surely children must think we are crazy that we can get sounds out of squiggles.

Children trust us so they try to make that madness happen. If they are lucky, they have patient adults that show them how the squiggles make sounds and that groups of squiggles combine to make words.

Part of the best way to help someone learn to read is to make sure they can hear the smallest sounds in words which are called phonemes. And before we can teach them the small sounds, we must make sure they can hear the big sounds.

So, the beginning of learning to read is making sure the student can hear words. That may seem silly since most people learn to talk when they are just babies. Yet if they haven't thought about what a word is, how can we expect them to turn squiggles into words?

This book will help your child, or even an adult learner, learn to hear each word in a sentence. Once they can do that, they must learn to hear syllables in each word. (Identifying syllables will also be an important skill when they are trying to read. Once they are taught the six types of syllables, it will make reading and writing a lot easier.) After they can identify the syllables in a word, it will be time to hear the individual sounds, the phonemes, in a word.

And then we tell them that each sound has a squiggle. If they put those squiggles together, they will make words. And if they can look at the squiggles someone has placed on a piece of paper or on a computer screen and they can make all those squiggles make a sound, they will have broken the squiggle code. That is when reading begins.

Table of Contents

Download DOG ON A LOG printable gameboards, games, flashcards, and other activities at:
www.dogonalogbooks.com/printables.

Parents and Teachers:
Receive email notifications of new books and printables. Sign up at:
www.dogonalogbooks.com/subscribe

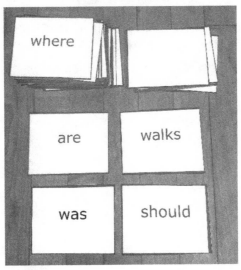

9

DOG ON A LOG
Parent and Teacher Guides

General Information
on Dyslexia and
Struggling Readers

The Author's Routine
for Teaching Reading

Book 1. *Teaching a Struggling Reader: One Mom's Experience with Dyslexia*

Book 2. *How to Use Decodable Books to Teach Reading*

Available for free from many online booksellers or read at: www.dogonalogbooks.com/free

Introduction

Humans naturally learn to walk and talk. These days, most of us learn to read. However, reading is not a natural process. For people to learn to do it well, most must be given direct instruction in how to do it.

Scientific research has shown that the best way for most people to learn to read is by using phonics.[1] The student learns to hear sounds in words then associates those sounds with squiggles that we call letters. Next, they learn to blend those letter sounds into words. If they are learning to read in English, they must also learn about all the different letter combinations that can sometimes make the same sounds. They must also learn about the words that do not follow the phonics rules.

Your child, or possibly an adult learner, learned to hear the sounds in words in *DOG ON A LOG Pup Book 1*: *Before the Squiggle Code (A Roadmap to Reading.)* If your child has not mastered the skills in that book, they are not ready for this book. As I pointed out in *Before the Squiggle Code*, you would not want someone to build your house if they put the roof on before the concrete floor was finished drying. The walls would sink into the concrete plus the foundation would be full of footprint impressions and nails that were dropped while the walls and roof were being built.

---

[1] *Put Reading First*, Third Edition, Center for the Improvement of Early Reading Achievement (CIERA) and funded by the National Institute for Literacy (NIFL)
https://lincs.ed.gov/publications/pdf/PRFbooklet.pdf

Once your child has mastered the skills from *Before the Squiggle Code (A Roadmap to Reading,)* it is time to start teaching your child about those squiggles they see in books, on the computer, or in your shopping list.

If you have not used *Before the Squiggle Code (A Roadmap to Reading,)* you may wish to make sure your child has mastered the pre-reading skills before starting this book. You can do this by using a phonemic awareness screening tool. I looked at several, but most are not written for parents. They can be easy to use, but they don't list by what age a child should be mastering a skill. As a parent, I found this screener the easiest to understand. It costs just a few dollars, to download: Phonemic Awareness and Dyslexia Screening Tool.[2] It can be used after the first 9 weeks of kindergarten.

This particular screening tool also includes asking children to say the names of letters. If they haven't been taught the letter names, (which is what they will learn in this book,) they would not, of course, get that portion of the assessment correct.

I have been told that, since every child develops at their own pace, it may be perfectly normal for kids to master any of these skills later than other children. However, if your child is still not mastering skills 6 to 12 months after other kids have mastered them, you should probably contact a dyslexia or learning disabilities specialist.

---

[2] https://www.teacherspayteachers.com/Product/Phonemic-Awareness-and-Dyslexia-Screening-4350750

Angie Neal, M.S., CCC-SLP, the developer of the tool messaged me, "These are average age ranges. That means it wouldn't be considered 'disordered' unless they are significantly behind. I would consider 6 months behind as delayed and a year or more behind as disordered. I would not consider one skill as a single predictor, but I would be sure to support development of that skill through reading and word play frequently."

The steps of learning to read aren't very complicated to outline. Like the first *Pup Book* in this series, this book is a roadmap. I will give you basic activities that will show you the progression your child needs to follow so they can break *The Squiggle Code*.

The roadmap outlined in this book is a good path for anyone learning to read. For typical learners, they may advance along the path rather quickly. Individuals with reading disabilities such as dyslexia may need additional learning strategies and a lot more repetition. However, *DOG ON A LOG Books* are written following a systematic Orton-Gillingham based phonics sequence and are perfect for individuals with dyslexia when they have the right guidance. (They are what my daughter with dyslexia reads.)

Please note, for someone with a learning disability such as dyslexia, learning to read is incredibly hard. Unlike most human brains that are receptive to learning to read, the brains of people with dyslexia just aren't wired to learn reading. They require a lot of repetition and usually do best when their lessons include activities that involve many senses. My daughter has dyslexia. The repetition she required, and continues to require, was often overwhelming for both her and me. However, by using a systematic phonics approach, her reading has steadily progressed.

This book draws upon my experiences of working with certified Orton-Gillingham teachers as well as the recommendations of professionals who specialize in phonics education and learning disabilities. However, coming up with strategies that can help individual learners is beyond what *DOG ON A LOG Books* are meant to do. I provide the roadmap and reading materials and the people that know your children can develop the methods for using the materials. A structured literacy program[3] such as the Orton-Gillingham Approach[4] is considered one of the best methods[5] for teaching children with dyslexia (and possibly most learners.) If your child is not progressing through and mastering the skills in this book, I highly recommend you seek guidance from a trained professional.

---

[3] https://dyslexiaida.org/what-is-structured-literacy/

[4] https://www.understood.org/en/school-learning/partnering-with-childs-school/instructional-strategies/orton-gillingham-research

[5] https://www.understood.org/en/school-learning/partnering-with-childs-school/instructional-strategies/orton-gillingham-what-you-need-to-know

Getting Help

Public school districts are required to provide information and resources to all children at no cost. Even if you are homeschooling, they must help your child. You can talk to the school psychologist or special education teacher about conducting a comprehensive evaluation. As I discussed in *Teaching a Struggling Reader: One Mom's Experience with Dyslexia,* not all schools provide adequate services for struggling readers. You will have to determine if you are satisfied with the services from your local school district.

Another option would be to contact a Learning Disabilities Specialist, Reading Specialist or teacher who is trained in using a structured Orton-Gillingham based approach. Sadly, private evaluations and tutoring are very expensive. Another option is to continue teaching your child by yourself. The road map in *DOG ON A LOG Books* is a systematic phonics sequence that will guide you in what to teach your child. However, it is not meant to instruct you in the finer aspects of teaching a child with a learning disability.

This surprised me, but Reading Specialists are not usually trained in working with students with dyslexia or other learning disabilities. If they are not trained in Orton-Gillingham instruction, they probably are not following the best scientifically-proven methods of teaching children with a reading disability.

You can learn more about struggling readers and dyslexia in my e-booklet *Teaching a Struggling Reader: One Mom's Experience with Dyslexia.* There is information about how to find the right type of specialist and how to find the information you need to help your child yourself.

Keeping this Affordable

Every family and child are different. If I included additional activities that some families enjoy while others do not, the production costs for all those extra pages would make this book more expensive. I know how hard it is to raise kids on a budget. To keep production costs of this book down, I limit the activities in *Pup Books*. These books show parents what skills their children must learn, then it is up to the parents to personalize the activities that work best for their children and themselves. You can find free or low-cost activities at many online sites including:

www.dogonalogbooks.com
www.pinterest.com
www.teacherspayteachers.com

I will also add that this is not a complete Orton-Gillingham based program. The amount of work involved in creating such a program would keep me from writing books for my daughter. Her books are my first priority. However, I know some families that cannot afford additional help so I am creating this roadmap for them.

There are many fine Orton-Gillingham based programs available for families and, if you can afford one, you may want to find one you like. However, production costs make those programs expensive.

In an ideal world, every school would provide the individualized attention each child needs. In an ideal world, every parent could afford private tutors. In an ideal world, the people who produce complete Orton-Gillingham based programs would not have to cover their own expenses and could just give their programs away for free.

I do not live in an ideal world, so I am creating this simple roadmap and making it available to the general public to try and make children's lives better. I try to keep it affordable for most families and, hopefully, it is available in your local library if your budget does not allow you to buy it.

Breaking the Squiggle Code

If your child has mastered the skills in *Before the Squiggle Code,* it is time to start them on the path towards decoding the squiggles they see all around them so they will actually begin to read.

We are going to introduce your child to the squiggles, also known as letters, and help them learn what each one says. In the English language there are 44 sounds called phonemes. In this book we will only introduce the five short vowel sounds and the 21 primary consonant sounds. The remaining 23 phonemes will be introduced in *DOG ON A LOG Let's GO! Books* and *DOG ON A LOG Chapter Books.*

My daughter learned most of her letter sounds from an online reading program called the Mindplay Virtual Reading Coach. It is a very good program that I can recommend for those who want online instruction. We decided we wanted more personalized assistance so hired a private Orton-Gillingham teacher. With the new teacher, our daughter continued learning the letter sounds with sound cards. Although you can buy good quality cards, I have created a set of cards that you can download from my website, www.dogonalogbook.com. If you laminate them, they should last a long time.

Most phonics programs introduce each letter with a keyword. A picture of the keyword will remind your child of the sound that letter makes. The keywords are introduced in this book. You can also print keyword cards and keyword tables from dogonalogbooks.com. My daughter has a 3-ring binder that contains her keyword tables. If she is having trouble remembering keywords, she consults her binder. (You can also tape them to the wall. I just don't choose to do that as I never know what room we'll be reading in.)

THIS IS IMPORTANT

When making the letter sounds, be careful to use clear sounds without adding "uh" at the end of the sound. If you say, "B says 'buh' and T says 'Tuh'" then ask your child to read b-a-t, they will probably say, "buh-a-tuh," instead of "bat." You may want to watch a video on how to correctly make each sound. One of my favorite videos for American pronunciations is by Cox Campus/Atlanta Speech School. Here is a direct link to view it on their website: https://app.coxcampus.org/#!/resourcelibrary/detail/5c38d865706cb4002d363755

You can also find a variety of international videos with local pronunciations on YouTube if you search for "44 Phonemes."

THIS IS IMPORTANT

Adapt to Your Child

This is so important it gets an entire page and two sets of arrows. This book is a roadmap. It shows you the skills your child must learn before they can proceed on the reading path. It also gives you ideas on how to introduce the skill and links to where you can find more activities. It is important that you use the activities and strategies that work for YOUR child. And if you have more than one child, you may need to use completely different strategies with each. When I have used this book while teaching at our homeschool co-op, I have found that sometimes I cannot follow the book exactly. That's okay because that's how kids learn. The book shows me what skill I need to teach so I find a different way of presenting it.

Of equal importance, the activities you use must also work for you. As bored as I was by doing sound cards over and over, that technique worked for my daughter. We also did the magnetic letters and played board games that had been adapted with "special cards" that were created for her reading level. At no time did I look on Pinterest for cute holiday-themed crafts that also taught letter sounds. I am not into crafts. My daughter is, so she does those types of activities at the homeschool co-operative or with her tutors, but not me. I just cannot stand doing crafts and I would have been miserable trying to find some then actually doing them. (Although if I was told the only way my daughter would ever read was by making construction paper stars, I would have done it. Fortunately, no one has said that.)

THIS IS IMPORTANT

You can skip some pages

If you roll your eyes when you see too much explanation, YOU CAN SKIP THE NEXT THREE PAGES OF THIS SECTION EXCEPT THE GREY BOXES. This is the outline you will use in the rest of the book. You will be given step-by-step instructions when you get to the activities.

These are the steps we use:

1. Show your child a letter in this book.

2. Say the name of the letter. Have the child repeat the letter's name.

3. Show your child how to trace the letter in the book. Have your child trace the letter.

4. State the keyword. The child will repeat the keyword.

5. Make the sound of the letter while tapping your pointer finger to your thumb. BE CAREFUL TO SAY THE SOUND CORRECTLY. Have the child repeat the sound of the letter while tapping their pointer finger to their thumb. (If you did not read about tapping in *Before the Squiggle Code*, that information is included in this book on page 74.)

21

6. Have them trace and/or draw the letter in a multisensory way. They can trace the letter from a printable sheet you can download from www.dogonalogbooks.com/printables or with glue/sand cards you make together or that you already conveniently made. Once your child can trace the letter, they can try and draw it with their fingers. You can have them draw it on a cookie sheet with shaving cream or sand (I would not recommend both at the same time) or whatever way you find works for you and your child.

7. Once your child has learned the first letter, it will be time to move onto the next letter, then the next.

8. When a group of letters has been introduced, and learned, it is time to start blending the sounds into words.

Let's Talk Repetition

For some children, learning a group of letters will be easy and they'll be ready to move on quickly. Other children may need repetition and fun activities that use many different senses. (We had to repeat the sound cards for weeks for our daughter who has dyslexia.) If you have repeated the first group of letters using a variety of activities over and over for many days or even weeks and your child is not progressing, this could be because they are young and their brains just aren't ready to learn this material. However, it is also possible they may have a learning disability such as dyslexia. If you suspect your child is not progressing as they should, you may want to seek out guidance. I've listed possible professionals to consult on page 15.

9. When your child is first starting to blend letters into words, it may work best for them to place their finger under each letter as they say the sounds. Have them say each sound as rapidly as they can until they create a word. It may work for you to demonstrate how a word is blended then let them imitate you. I will also discuss using a Magical Magnetic Bingo Wand when we get to the section on blending.

10. Once they get the concept of blending sounds to make words, I highly recommend they be taught to tap every letter sound as they read each word. There are tapping instructions on page 74. When my daughter cannot figure out a word, tapping helps her focus. She can't bring in extra sounds or lose sounds if she is tapping the sounds she sees in print.

11. You can have your child read the words, sentences, and stories in this book. Some kids are overwhelmed by too many pages and words all at once. It may be easier to use the printable sheets and flashcards on my website and/or buy *Kids' Squiggles (Letters Make Words)* which contains the stories in a more child-friendly format.

12. After your child is able to sound out (decode) words, sight words will be introduced. Instructions on how to teach sight words will be discussed on page 80 of this book. Sight words are words that cannot be decoded because they simply do not follow phonics rules or because the rules they do follow have not been introduced yet.

13. It is important to incorporate writing and reading the learned sounds/rules/sight words at each step of the way. Don't just focus on the rules, they need to actually practice reading and writing.

DOWNLOADABLE PRINTABLES

Here is a partial list of printables available on my website, www.dogonalogbooks.com/printables. You will find the following printables that you can use with the lessons in this book and other DOG ON A LOG Books.

At the time of writing, my local library prints color pages for ten cents a page so that's where I print the gameboards and materials we use at home.

- Free printable Gameboards that can be adapted to your child by using the flashcards your child is currently using.
- Gamecards you can personalize (Word docx and/or PDF formats.) This allows you to play the boardgames even if you do NOT follow the DOG ON A LOG Phonics Progression.
- Letter cards for tracing. D'Nealian font.
- Keyword cards (letter plus keyword picture) and Alphabet Cards (just the letter) in various combinations of just lower case, lower case and capital, or just capital letter.
- Keyword tables to place in a binder or tape to the wall.
- Word Cards and Sentence Cards with the words and sentences in this book. Tup is on the back so they can be used as gamecards.
- Traceable sight word strips.
- Sight word flashcards.
- Printable handwriting worksheets. (The sentences only use sight words with letters that have been previously introduced for handwriting.)
- Handwriting paper with various sizes of lines.
- "Tup Money" for motivation.
- Printable PDF Bookfold version of the words and sentences from this book

Other Useful Materials

Before the Squiggle Code: A Roadmap to Reading, (If your child has NOT mastered the early skills presented in that book.)

Kids' Squiggles (Letters Make Words) contains all the stories included in this book in a more child-friendly format.

Magnetic Bingo Wand with metal chips (choking hazard so do not get if you have a child at risk.) Instructions for use on page 59.

Printable word list, sentences, sound cards, gameboards, etc. as listed on page 24.

A **laminator** with **laminating pouches** (if you want to make the printable materials more durable.)

Magnetic Letters let you create words faster than you can probably write them. Various reading programs sell magnetic letters with a board they stick to. However, if they are out of your budget and you have refrigerator magnets with letters and a large cookie sheet, you can give that a try. You can also create words with printable alphabet cards that are available to download from my website; just set the cards down next to each other on a table or other surface.

Small Erasable White Board with Guide Lines for Writing and **Dry Erase Markers** let your child write without having to use so much paper.

Wet Erase Markers are similar to dry erase markers except you have to use water to erase. For use personalizing laminated pdf gamecards/flashcards.

Let's Talk Motivation

Learning to read can be really hard and often kids just don't see the purpose of all that work. I highly recommend finding a reward you can offer your child for their hard work.

My daughter's first teacher rewarded every effort she made. She wasn't rewarded for getting the correct answer; she was rewarded for trying. My daughter earned play money, typically $1 for every attempt she made. Often, she'd earn $100 or more in a single reading session. I kept small items in a "treasure box" at the teacher's office. They were usually trinkets I got at the dollar store or a thrift shop. At the end of the session, my daughter got to buy something from the treasure box (gosh, most items were no more than $100 so she could get something after each session.) Eventually, she started saving her money so she could "buy" something big. Each session she would buy two yogurt covered pretzels for $10 so she got an instant reward, then she saved the rest of her play money. Interestingly, at home she wanted to use playing cards to reward her attempts. She didn't want to buy anything with them, she just wanted the acknowledgement that she had tried. In time, her reward at home became a piece of gum.

She has since outgrown needing immediate rewards, but getting them was really important during the first year or so.

The mascot dog for this book series is named Tup. I have created "Tup Money" that you can download and print from my website if your child needs play money as a motivator.

Let's Talk Patience

Children want to please. They especially want to please their parents. If your child is struggling with reading or trying to avoid it, or is sitting on their head trying to read upside-down, it is probably because learning to read is hard and maybe boring.

When my daughter acts this way, I often have to take a deep breath and count to 100.

From time to time I want to scream, "Just read the stupid story!!!!" Fortunately, I am able to control myself. Most of the time.

You and your child will be much happier and make better progress if you remain positive. Reward them by saying, "Good job," "I can see you're trying so hard," or "I am so proud of how hard you are working. I know this is really hard," over and over.

And, as I said before, find a motivating reward. After a lot of trial and error, I found what really motivated my daughter more than anything else was simply a piece of gum.

If you and your child are struggling, find what helps you to stay calm and patient. Your emotions will ultimately determine the emotions you both feel. If you are calm, your child will eventually calm down. If you are frustrated, your child will get even more frustrated and frustrating

Remember, you are not the only parent who has been frustrated. And, remember, with the right interventions, your child will learn to read.

The Squiggles are also Called:

Letters

In this book, I call letters "capitals" and "lowercase." These are the terms 100% of the homeschooling parents I surveyed said they use. They use "capital" rather than "uppercase" because they tell their children, "You need to capitalize that," so they want them to know the word, "capital." They did not like the terms "big and small letters" because that can refer to font size.

Font

Font is how a letter looks. Here is the letter "a" in three different fonts:

a   a   *a*

This book is typed with Verdana font which research has shown is one of the most dyslexia-friendly fonts. My daughter was taught handwriting with the D'Nealian font. It is pretty and it her teachers all feel it is easier to write. I was going to use D'Nealian tracing font in this book. However, in the large size I use for tracing, some of the letters look quite different than the rest of the typed letters. I have therefore decided to use a more standard block print for tracing in the body of the book. There are block capital letters and D'Nealian letters for tracing at the back of the book should you want to use them. Your child needs to learn handwriting as they learn the letters. You can download handwriting worksheets from dogonalogbooks.com/printables.

Your child may benefit from starting with the downloadable/printable Keyword Cards available at www.dogonalogbooks.com/printables. These are cards with the letter and the keyword picture.

Your child should be taught:

- The name of the letter.
- The keyword.
- The sound the letter makes.

Once they have memorized the keyword for a letter, you will want to switch to the sound cards (without the pictures.) This will help them learn to state the keyword and letter sound from memory without having to see the picture, such as saying: a, apple, /a./ (When a letter is in brackets, it means to say the letter sound, not the letter name.)

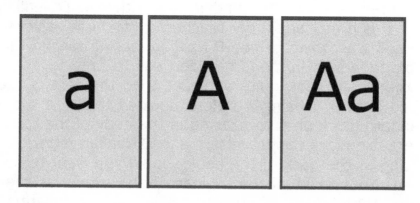

Letter Group 1

a, s, m, f, t, n

Sight Words Introduced:
the, is

Vowel: a

We learned to clap syllables in *Before the Squiggle Code*.

Tell your child, "Every syllable has a vowel. We will get to meet the vowels one by one.

"The first vowel is…"

- Show your child this letter.
- Say the name of this letter.
- Have your child repeat the letter's name.
- Show your child how to trace the letter.
- Have your child trace the letter.

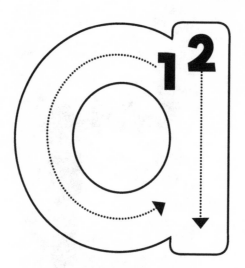

- Tell your child, "The name of this letter is 'a.' Its keyword is apple."
- Have your child repeat the keyword.
- Tell your child, "The letter 'a' says /a/ just like the beginning sound in apple."
- Touch your pointer finger to your thumb and say, /a./
- Have your child touch their pointer finger to their thumb and repeat the sound /a./
- Have your child trace or draw the letter in a fun, multisensory way.

- Tell your child, "Just like you look different if you change your clothes, 'a' can look different if it changes its clothes. These are both the letter 'a.'"
- The first way we see 'a' is easier to write.
- The second way we see 'a' is how it often looks when it is in a book or has been typed on a computer.

a   a

When we write sentences or names, we start them with superhero letters which we call "Capital Letters." Capital letters are like Superheroes. They do great things when they put on their special clothes. This is what an 'a' looks like when it puts on its super "Capital Clothes:"

A

This is a capital 'A' and a lowercase 'a' typed on a computer.

Aa

You may wish to show your child the downloadable/printable Capital letter card.

- Show your child this letter.
- Say the name of this letter.
- Have your child repeat the letter's name.
- Show your child how to trace the letter.
- Have your child trace the letter.

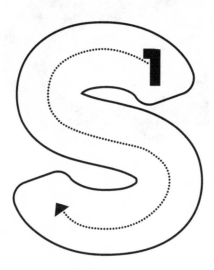

- Tell your child, "The name of this letter is 's.' Its keyword is snake."
- Have your child repeat the keyword. You may want to show them the keyword card and keyword table.
- Tell your child, "The letter 's' says /s/ just like the beginning sound in snake."
- Touch your pointer finger to your thumb and say, /s./
- Have your child touch their pointer finger to their thumb and repeat the sound /s./
- Have your child trace or draw the letter in a fun, multisensory way.

When we write sentences or names, we start them with capital letters. This is what a capital 'S' looks like.

S

This is a Capital 'S' and a lowercase 's' typed on a computer.

Ss

You may wish to show your child the Capital Letter Card from www.dogonalogbooks.com/printables.

- Show your child this letter.
- Say the name of this letter.
- Have your child repeat the letter's name.
- Show your child how to trace the letter.
- Have your child trace the letter.

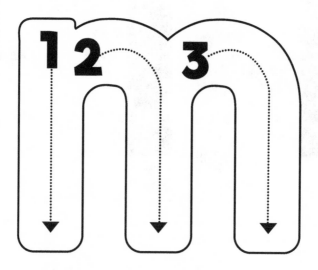

- Tell your child, "The name of this letter is 'm.' Its keyword is man." You may want to show them the keyword card and keyword table.
- Have your child repeat the keyword. You may want to show them the keyword card and keyword table.
- Tell your child, "The letter 'm' says /m/ just like the beginning sound in man."
- Touch your pointer finger to your thumb and say, /m./
- Have your child touch their pointer finger to their thumb and repeat the sound /m./
- Have your child trace or draw the letter in a fun, multisensory way.

When we write sentences or names, we start them with capital letters. This is what a capital 'M' looks like.

M

This is a Capital 'M' and a lowercase 'm' typed on a computer.

Mm

You may wish to show your child the Capital Letter Card from www.dogonalogbooks.com/printables.

- Show your child this letter.
- Say the name of this letter.
- Have your child repeat the letter's name.
- Show your child how to trace the letter.
- Have your child trace the letter.

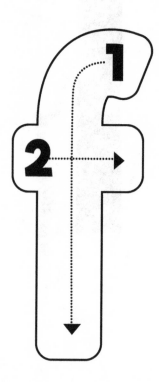

- Tell your child, "The name of this letter is 'f.' Its keyword is fun."
- Have your child repeat the keyword. You may want to show them the keyword card and keyword table.
- Tell your child, "The letter 'f' says /f/ just like the beginning sound in fun."
- Touch your pointer finger to your thumb and say, /f./
- Have your child touch their pointer finger to their thumb and repeat the sound /f./
- Have your child trace or draw the letter in a fun, multisensory way.

When we write sentences or names, we start them with capital letters. This is what a capital 'F' looks like.

F

This is a Capital 'F' and a lowercase 'f' typed on a computer.

Ff

You may wish to show your child the Capital Letter Card from www.dogonalogbooks.com/printables.

- Show your child this letter.
- Say the name of this letter.
- Have your child repeat the letter's name.
- Show your child how to trace the letter.
- Have your child trace the letter.

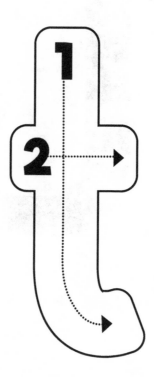

- Tell your child, "The name of this letter is 't.' Its keyword is top."
- Have your child repeat the keyword. You may want to show them the keyword card and keyword table.
- Tell your child, "The letter 't' says /t/ just like the beginning sound in top."
- Touch your pointer finger to your thumb and say, /t./
- Have your child touch their pointer finger to their thumb and repeat the sound /t./
- Have your child trace or draw the letter in a fun, multisensory way.

When we write sentences or names, we start them with capital letters. This is what a capital 'T' looks like.

T

This is a Capital 'T' and a lowercase 't' typed on a computer.

Tt

You may wish to show your child the Capital Letter Card from www.dogonalogbooks.com/printables.

- Show your child this letter.
- Say the name of this letter.
- Have your child repeat the letter's name.
- Show your child how to trace the letter.
- Have your child trace the letter.

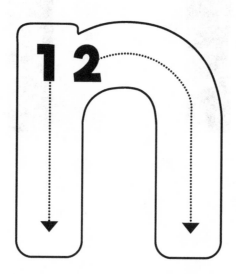

- Tell your child, "The name of this letter is 'n.' Its keyword is nut."
- Have your child repeat the keyword. You may want to show them the keyword card and keyword table.
- Tell your child, "The letter 'n' says /n/ just like the beginning sound in nut."
- Touch your pointer finger to your thumb and say, /n./
- Have your child touch their pointer finger to their thumb and repeat the sound /n./
- Have your child trace or draw the letter in a fun, multisensory way.

When we write sentences or names, we start them with capital letters. This is what a capital 'N' looks like.

N

This is a Capital 'N' and a lowercase 'n' typed on a computer.

Nn

You may wish to show your child the Capital Letter Card from www.dogonalogbooks.com/printables.

When your child has memorized the letters **a, s, m, f, t, n** it is time to move on to blending. If your child needs reminders of the sound any letter makes, ask them to tell you the keyword and the letter's sound. If they do not remember it, show them a keyword card or keep a binder with keyword tables available for them to look at.

For my daughter, practice was sitting on her swing while I showed her a sound card and said, "Tell me the name of the letter, its keyword, and its sound." I cannot tell you how many times we did this as it seemed to go on forever. It took weeks, maybe longer. I am not exaggerating. It was excruciatingly painful. And she had actually mastered a lot of the letters over the course of a year while doing MindPlay Virtual Reading Coach so she did not have to memorize all 26 letters using the sound cards.

Blending Words

Magical Magnetic Bingo Wand

Many children grasp the idea of blending if you demonstrate with a magnetic bingo wand. This is a wand with a magnet that comes with plastic chips that contain a small bit of metal. They are fairly inexpensive and can be purchased online. (Search Magnetic Bingo Wand.)

Place a chip on a surface for each letter in a word. If you have a grid to set them on, great. Otherwise just set them on a table or desk. If you have two colors of chips, you can make the vowel a different color chip.

Have the child say the sound of each letter then pick up the wand and wave it over the chips as they say the word. The wand will grab all the chips together just as saying the word will blend the letters together. For many children, this really cements the concept of blending.

Ask your child to say each of these sounds while tapping their pointer finger to their thumb. Do not ask them to blend the sounds.

a

m

Now ask your child to place their fingers under each letter and say each sound.

Ask them to repeat this as quickly as they can until they say the word "am."

If they do not understand what you are asking them to do, demonstrate this then have them copy you.

Once your child understands that saying the letter sounds quickly will help them read a word, you should celebrate. THEY JUST READ THEIR FIRST WORD!!!

Ask your child to say each of these sounds while tapping their pointer finger to their thumb. Do not ask them to blend the sounds.

a

t

Now ask your child to place their fingers under each letter and say each sound.

Ask them to repeat this as quickly as they can until they say the word "at."

If they do not understand what you are asking them to do, demonstrate this then have them copy you.

Ask your child to say each of these sounds while tapping their pointer finger to their thumb. Do not ask them to blend the sounds.

m

a

n

Now ask your child to place their fingers under each letter and say each sound.

Ask them to repeat this as quickly as they can until they say the word "man."

If they do not understand what you are asking them to do, demonstrate this then have them copy you.

Ask your child to say each of these sounds while tapping their pointer finger to their thumb. Do not ask them to blend the sounds.

s

a

t

Now ask your child to place their fingers under each letter and say each sound.

Ask them to repeat this as quickly as they can until they say the word "sat."

If they do not understand what you are asking them to do, demonstrate this then have them copy you.

sat

Ask your child to say each of these sounds while tapping their pointer finger to their thumb. Do not ask them to blend the sounds.

m

a

t

Now ask your child to place their fingers under each letter and say each sound.

Ask them to repeat this as quickly as they can until they say the word "mat."

If they do not understand what you are asking them to do, demonstrate this then have them copy you.

Ask your child to say each of these sounds while tapping their pointer finger to their thumb. Do not ask them to blend the sounds.

f

a

n

Now ask your child to place their fingers under each letter and say each sound.

Ask them to repeat this as quickly as they can until they say the word "fan."

If they do not understand what you are asking them to do, demonstrate this then have them copy you.

fan

Congratulations on reading all those words. Good job!!!

It is almost time to read words with capital letters. You can download printable Capital Letter Cards from www.dogonalogbooks.com/printables.

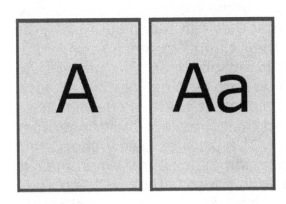

Review the lowercase and capital letters below. You may wish to keep the Capital Letter cards near your child so they can refer to them if they need to. There are traceable capital letters starting on page 276.

Aa, Ss, Mm, Ff, Tt, Nn

Tapping

Tapping is one of the most useful skills a new reader can learn. Now that they can sound out words, they will "tap" a finger to their thumb for each sound in a word. This makes it multisensory. It is also harder to lose track of the letters if you are tapping your fingers for each sound. For the remainder of the activities in this book, have your child tap their thumb to their finger for each sound in the words. The pictures below show which finger to tap for each sound in the word. When they start tapping words with four sounds, they will tap the pinkie. For longer words they tap through the pinkie then start over with the pointer finger.

TAPPING: First sound in a word

TAPPING:
Second
sound
in a
word

TAPPING:
Third
sound
in a
word

Reading Words

Have your child decode (sound out) these words. Some of these words are names. Names start with Capital Letters. Have your child tap and sound out these words. They can also be downloaded in a pdf bookfold, 8.5 x 11 sheet, or flashcards that can be used as gamecards with any of the DOG ON A LOG gameboards.

am   an   man

sat   tan   mat

fan   fat   Nan

Tam   Sam

Here are some silly words your child can sound out. Sounding out silly words is a good skill because it means they are not guessing.

nam   fam

If you have a magnetic letter board, you and your child can play with the letters. One of you can make a word, have the child tap and sound it out, then change a letter, and sound out the new word. If you don't have a magnetic board, you can use the sound cards. Using these tools is easier than writing them out all the time. Exchanging letters helps a child understand that the sounds and word meanings change when the letters change.

Writing

It is important that your child practice writing along with practicing reading. They need multiple senses involved to cement these new skills. They also need to learn how to write.

Ask your child to write a few of the words from the prior page. You can download printable lined paper at www.dogonalogbooks.com/printables. To avoid using so much paper, you can also get a white board with guide lines and dry erase markers. Kids should still practice on paper as I have been told some don't always transfer their skills from the white board to paper. However, the white board is one more way to practice.

Time to Rhyme

Let's make rhymes by changing the first letter of the following words.

Read this word:

man

Let's change the first letter to "f."

Read this word:

fan

Let's change the first letter to "t."

Read this word:

tan

You can use magnetic letter boards or sound cards to play this game. Create silly words or real words.

Switch the End

What happens if we change the last letter?

Read this word:

fan

Let's change the last letter to "t."

Read this word:

fat

Let's change the last letter to "m."

Read this silly word:

fam

You can use magnetic letter boards or sound cards to play this game. Create silly words or real words.

Sight Words

There are two meanings for the term "sight words." One is any word that is recognized instantly at sight. The other is a word that has an irregular element, such as the "ai" in the word said.

DOG ON A LOG Books designate sight words throughout the series for one of two reasons:
    1. They do not follow regular phonics rules.
    2. The phonics rule has not been taught yet.

Memorizing words that do not follow known phonics rules can be very difficult for some children. There are many ways to learn sight words. This is the approach my daughter's first tutor taught us. She made traceable letter strips by writing 2-inch tall words on strips of paper grocery bags. You can download and print Sight Word Tracing Strips from www.dogonalogbooks.com/printables.

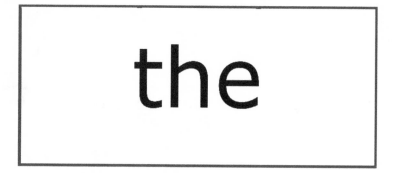

The process for using these strips:

1. With two fingers, the child underlines the word while saying the word.
2. With two fingers the student traces each letter while saying the letter's name.
3. They underline the word again while saying it.

4. Pause for a moment then start the whole process over.
5. Repeat this until the student feels they can write the word.
6. Write the word on paper or a dry erase board then verify its spelling.
7. Write it again and verify the spelling.
8. Write each word a minimum of 5 times.
9. Once the word is memorized, its flashcard is added to the daily flashcard stack.

Sometimes this is all that is needed. Other words require us to do this procedure multiple times. I have been told some kids will have to trace a complicated word at least 100 times to learn it. Dyslexia requires lots of repetition.

You may find different sight word activities that you and your child prefer at www.pinterest.com or www.teacherspayteachers.com. You can download a gameboard from dogonalogbooks.com/printables and read the sight word flashcards when you land on the "Read to Tup" spots.

Sight Words for Sentences

Please help your child learn the following sight words. You can use the above method or a method of your choice.

the

is

Story Time

Have your child read the story on the next page. They should tap each sound. Make sure they tap the correct fingers as this will help them when words get longer and more complicated.

First sound: Tap pointer finger to thumb.
Second sound: Tap middle finger to thumb.
Third sound: Tap ring finger to thumb.

If your child cannot remember a letter's sound, ask them the keyword. If that does not help them remember the sound, show them the keyword card or table.

Your child may be less intimidated by all the words on the page if you use a paper to cover the sentences below where your child is reading.

Pace yourself. If your child is struggling, just read a sentence or two. Congratulate them for their hard work (because this IS hard for them.) If your child is still able to proceed, trace the letters, play games finding objects that have the same beginning, ending, or middle letter. Come back to this when your child is ready.

If your child would prefer to read the story from a kid-friendly book, the stories are available in *Kids' Squiggles (Letters Make Words.)*

Nan Fam

Nan Fam is tan.

Nan Fam sat.

Tan Nan Fam sat.

Sam is the man.

The man is Sam Fam.

Sam Fam sat.

Sam Fam the man sat.

Sam Fam is the man.

Letter Group 2

r, d, c, g

Sight Words Introduced:
a, and, to, has

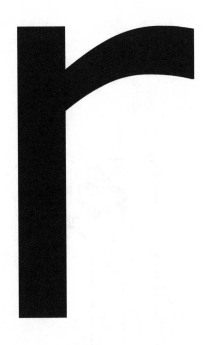

- Show your child this letter.
- Say the name of this letter.
- Have your child repeat the letter's name.
- Show your child how to trace the letter.
- Have your child trace the letter.

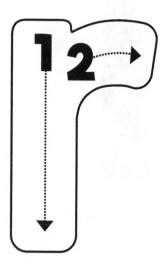

- Tell your child, "The name of this letter is 'r.' Its keyword is rat."
- Have your child repeat the keyword.
- Tell your child, "The letter 'r' says /r/ just like the beginning sound in rat."
- Touch your pointer finger to your thumb and say, /r./
- Have your child touch their pointer finger to their thumb and repeat the sound /r./
- Have your child trace or draw the letter in a fun, multisensory way.

When we write sentences or names, we start them with capital letters. This is what a capital 'R' looks like.

R

This is a Capital 'R' and a lowercase 'r' typed on a computer.

Rr

You may wish to show your child the Capital Letter Card from www.dogonalogbooks.com/printables.

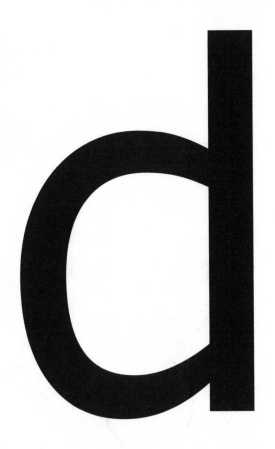

- Show your child this letter.
- Say the name of this letter.
- Have your child repeat the letter's name.
- Show your child how to trace the letter.
- Have your child trace the letter.

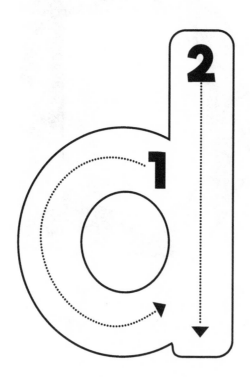

- Tell your child, "The name of this letter is 'd.' Its keyword is dog."
- Have your child repeat the keyword.
- Tell your child, "The letter 'd' says /d/ just like the beginning sound in dog."
- Touch your pointer finger to your thumb and say, /d./
- Have your child touch their pointer finger to their thumb and repeat the sound /d./
- Have your child trace or draw the letter in a fun, multisensory way.

When we write sentences or names, we start them with capital letters. This is what a capital 'D' looks like.

D

This is a Capital 'D' and a lowercase 'd' typed on a computer.

Dd

You may wish to show your child the Capital Letter Card from www.dogonalogbooks.com/printables.

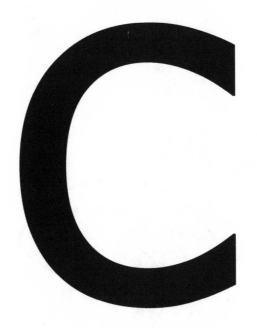

- Show your child this letter.
- Say the name of this letter.
- Have your child repeat the letter's name.
- Show your child how to trace the letter.
- Have your child trace the letter.

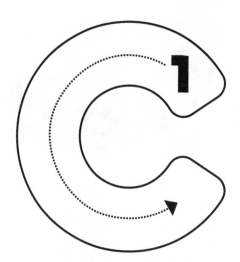

- Tell your child, "The name of this letter is 'c.' Its keyword is cat." You may want to show them the keyword card and keyword table.
- Have your child repeat the keyword.
- Tell your child, "The letter 'c' says /c/ just like the beginning sound in cat."
- Touch your pointer finger to your thumb and say, /c./
- Have your child touch their pointer finger to their thumb and repeat the sound /c./
- Have your child trace or draw the letter in a fun, multisensory way.

When we write sentences or names, we start them with capital letters. This is what a capital 'C' looks like.

C

This is a Capital 'C' and a lowercase 'c' typed on a computer.

Cc

You may wish to show your child the Capital Letter Card from www.dogonalogbooks.com/printables.

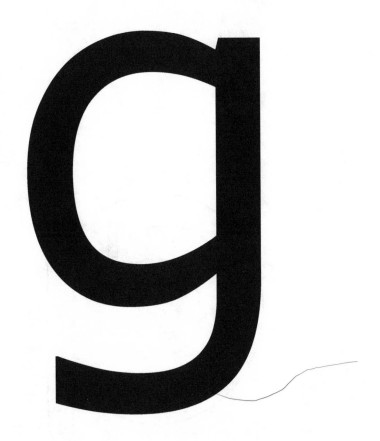

- Show your child this letter.
- Say the name of this letter.
- Have your child repeat the letter's name.
- Show your child how to trace the letter.
- Have your child trace the letter.

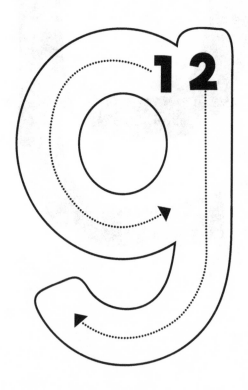

- Tell your child, "The name of this letter is 'g.' Its keyword is game." You may want to show them the keyword card and keyword table.
- Have your child repeat the keyword.
- Tell your child, "The letter 'g' says /g/ just like the beginning sound in game."
- Touch your pointer finger to your thumb and say, /g./
- Have your child touch their pointer finger to their thumb and repeat the sound /g./
- Have your child trace or draw the letter in a fun, multisensory way.

The lowercase 'g' can look different depending on how a computer is instructed to make it look. Here are two ways "g" can look when it is typed:

g   g

When we write sentences or names, we start them with capital letters. This is what a capital 'G' looks like.

G

This is a Capital 'G' and a lowercase 'g' typed on a computer. This is the lowercase 'g' that we use in this book.

Gg

You may wish to show your child the Capital Letter Card from www.dogonalogbooks.com/printables.

Blending Words

Ask your child to say each of these sounds while tapping their pointer finger to their thumb. Do not ask them to blend the sounds.

r

a

m

Now ask your child to place their fingers under each letter and say each sound.

Ask them to repeat this as quickly as they can until they say the word "ram."

If they do not understand what you are asking them to do, demonstrate this then have them copy you.

Ask your child to say each of these sounds while tapping their pointer finger to their thumb. Do not ask them to blend the sounds.

r

a

g

Now ask your child to place their fingers under each letter and say each sound.

Ask them to repeat this as quickly as they can until they say the word "rag."

If they do not understand what you are asking them to do, demonstrate this then have them copy you.

Review the lowercase and capital letters below. You may wish to keep the Capital Letter cards near your child so they can refer to them if they need to.

Rr, Dd, Cc, Gg

Reading Words

Have your child decode (sound out) these words. Some of these words are names. Names start with Capital Letters. Have your child tap and sound out these words. They can also be downloaded in a pdf bookfold, 8.5 x 11 sheet, or flashcards that can be used as gamecards with any of the DOG ON A LOG gameboards.

ram   rat   ran

tag   sag   cat

can   gas   fad

Dan   Tad   Dad

Here are some silly words your child can sound out. Sounding out silly words is a good skill because it means they are not guessing.

gat   nad   cag

If you have a magnetic letter board, you and your child can play with the letters to make real or silly words. Take time to substitute one letter at a time so your child can see how you make new words by changing the letters. If you don't have a magnetic board, you can use the sound cards to create words.

Writing

It is important that your child practice writing along with practicing reading. They need multiple senses involved to cement these new skills. They also need to learn how to write.

Ask your child to write a few of the words from the prior page. You can download printable lined paper at www.dogonalogbooks.com/printables. To avoid using so much paper, you can also get a white board with guide lines and dry erase markers. Kids should still practice on paper as I have been told some don't always transfer their skills from the white board to paper. However, the white board is one more way to practice.

Time to Rhyme

Let's make rhymes by changing the first letter of the following words.

Read this word:

tag

Let's change the first letter to "r."

Read this word:

rag

Let's change the first letter to "s."

Read this word:

sag

You can use magnetic letter boards or sound cards to play this game. Create silly words or real words.

Switch the End

What happens if we change the last letter?

Read this word:

ram

Let's change the last letter to "t."

Read this word:

rat

Let's change the last letter to "g."

Read this word:

rag

You can use magnetic letter boards or sound cards to play this game. Create silly words or real words.

Sight Words for Sentences

Please help your child learn the following sight words. You can use the method on page 80 or a method of your choice.

You will notice that the word "and" is included as a sight word. Because it is a consonant blend, it has not been introduced as a word for your child to sound out yet. It is being introduced as a sight word. Consonant blends are introduced in Step 4 of DOG ON A LOG Chapter and Let's GO! Books.

a

and

to

has

Sentence Time

Have your child read the sentences on the next page. They should tap each sound. Make sure they tap the correct fingers.

First sound: Tap pointer finger to thumb.
Second sound: Tap middle finger to thumb.
Third sound: Tap ring finger to thumb.

If your child cannot remember a letter's sound, ask them the keyword. If that does not help them remember the sound, show them the keyword card or table.

It may be easier at first if you hide all the sentences below what your child is reading. You can do this by covering them with a piece of paper.

Pace yourself. If your child is struggling, just read a sentence or two. Congratulate them for their hard work (because this IS hard for them.) If your child is still able to proceed, trace the letters, play games finding objects that have the same beginning, ending, or middle letter. Come back to this when your child is ready.

If your child would prefer to read the sentences from a "book," they are available as downloadable printable bookfold pdfs at www.dogonalogbooks.com/printables. They can also be downloaded in list form on 8.5 x 11 paper.

1. Dan has a mat and a can.

2. Dad is sad and Dan is mad.

3. Sam the rat ran to Dan.

4. Tam the cat ran.

5. Can Dan tag Tad and Dad?

6. Tad the tan ram ran to Tam.

7. The sad rat has gas.

8. Tad the ram ran to the dam.

Story Time

If your child would prefer to read the story from a kid-friendly book, the stories are available in *Kids' Squiggles (Letters Make Words.)*

Tag

Dan has a cat.

The cat is Tam.

Tam the cat ran.

Dan ran to tag Tad.

Tad is a ram.

Tad the ram ran to tag Dad.

Dad ran.

Dan ran to tag Tam the cat.

Tam the cat ran and ran.

Letter Group 3

O

Vowel: o

Remind your child, "Every syllable has a vowel. We will get to meet the vowels one by one.

"The second vowel we will meet is..."

- Show your child this letter.
- Say the name of this letter.
- Have your child repeat the letter's name.
- Show your child how to trace the letter.
- Have your child trace the letter.

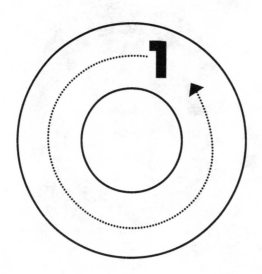

- Tell your child, "The name of this letter is 'o.' Its keyword is octopus." You may want to show them the keyword card and keyword table.
- Have your child repeat the keyword.
- Tell your child, "The letter 'o' says /o/ just like the beginning sound in octopus."
- Touch your pointer finger to your thumb and say, /o./
- Have your child touch their pointer finger to their thumb and repeat the sound /o./
- Have your child trace or draw the letter in a fun, multisensory way.

When we write sentences or names, we start them with capital letters. This is what a capital 'O' looks like.

O

This is a Capital 'O' and a lowercase 'o' typed on a computer.

Oo

You may wish to show your child the Capital Letter Card from www.dogonalogbooks.com/printables.

Reading Words

Have your child decode (sound out) these words. Some of these words are names. Names start with Capital Letters. Have your child tap and sound out these words. They can also be downloaded in a pdf bookfold, 8.5 x 11 sheet, or flashcards that can be used as gamecards with any of the DOG ON A LOG gameboards.

on	sod	tot
not	nod	cod
cog	rod	dot
dog	cot	got
Don	Ron	Tom

Here are some silly words your child can sound out. Sounding out silly words is a good skill because it means they are not guessing.

gom	mog	fod

If you have a magnetic letter board, you and your child can play with the letters to make real or silly words. Take time to substitute one letter at a time so your child can see how you make new words by changing the letters. If you don't have a magnetic board, you can use the sound cards to create words.

Writing

It is important that your child practice writing along with practicing reading. They need multiple senses involved to cement these new skills. They also need to learn how to write.

Ask your child to write a few of the words from the prior page. You can download printable lined paper at www.dogonalogbooks.com/printables. To avoid using so much paper, you can also get a white board with guide lines and dry erase markers. Kids should still practice on paper as I have been told some don't always transfer their skills from the white board to paper. However, the white board is one more way to practice.

Time to Rhyme

Let's make rhymes by changing the first letter of the following words.

Read this word:

dot

Let's change the first letter to "c."

Read this word:

cot

Let's change the first letter to "n."

not

You can use magnetic letter boards or sound cards to play this game. Create silly words or real words.

Switch the End

What happens if we change the last letter?

Read this word:

cod

Let's change the last letter to "t."

Read this word:

cot

Let's change the last letter to "g."

Read this word:

cog

You can use magnetic letter boards or sound cards to play this game. Create silly words or real words.

Change the Middle

What happens if we change the middle letter?

Read this word:

cat

Let's change the middle letter to "o."

Read this word:

cot

Let's try a different word. Read this word:

tag

Let's change the middle letter to "o."

Read this word:

tog

You can use magnetic letter boards or sound cards to play this game. Create silly words or real words.

Sentence Time

Have your child read the sentences on the next page. They should tap each sound. Make sure they tap the correct fingers.

First sound: Tap pointer finger to thumb.
Second sound: Tap middle finger to thumb.
Third sound: Tap ring finger to thumb.

If your child cannot remember a letter's sound, ask them the keyword. If that does not help them remember the sound, show them the keyword card or table.

It may be easier at first if you hide all the sentences below what your child is reading. You can do this by covering them with a piece of paper.

Pace yourself. If your child is struggling, just read a sentence or two. Congratulate them for their hard work (because this IS hard for them.) If your child is still able to proceed, trace the letters, play games finding objects that have the same beginning, ending, or middle letter. Come back to this when your child is ready.

If your child would prefer to read the sentences from a "book," they are available as downloadable printable bookfold pdfs at www.dogonalogbooks.com/printables.

1. Tom got a dog and a cat.

2. Don has a cot on a mat.

3. Ron is not a tot.

4. Ron is the dad to Don.

5. Ron ran to Tam the cat.

6. The dog ran on sod and Tom got mad.

7. Don sat on the cot.

8. Tam the cat sat on the sod.

Story Time

If your child would prefer to read the story from a kid-friendly book, the stories are available in *Kids' Squiggles (Letters Make Words.)*

The Tot

Don is a tot.

Don sat on a cat.

Don sat on a cod.

The cat got mad.

The cod got mad.

Don is sad.

Don got the cat a mat.

Don got the cod a cot.

The cat is not mad.

The cod is not mad.

Don is not sad.

Letter Group 4

b, h, l, x

Sight Words Introduced:
does, go, of

- Show your child this letter.
- Say the name of this letter.
- Have your child repeat the letter's name.
- Show your child how to trace the letter.
- Have your child trace the letter. My daughter was taught to make small "b" this way: **Start at the top, go down the stem, then go around up the belly. This is very different from how "d" is made, so it will help children who confuse "b" and "d."**

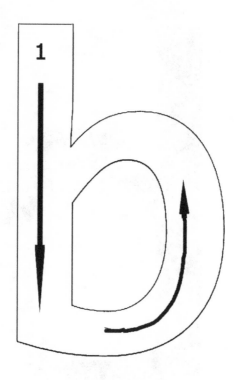

- Tell your child, "The name of this letter is 'b.' Its keyword is bat."
- Have your child repeat the keyword.
- Tell your child, "The letter 'b' says /b/ just like the beginning sound in bat."
- Touch your pointer finger to your thumb and say, /b./
- Have your child touch their pointer finger to their thumb and repeat the sound /b./
- Have your child trace or draw the letter in a fun, multisensory way.

- These are both the letter 'b.'"
- The first way we see 'b' is easier to write.
- The second way we see 'b' with a little stem at the bottom. This is how it often looks when it has been typed on a computer.

b   b

When we write sentences or names, we start them with capital letters. This is what a capital 'B' looks like.

B

This is a Capital 'B' and a lowercase 'b' typed on a computer.

Bb

You may wish to show your child the Capital Letter Card from www.dogonalogbooks.com/printables.

Letter Reversals

Letter Reversals

Lowercase "b" "d" "p" "g" and "q" can look alike to many children. Depending on the font, if you rotate these letters, they could all be the same shape. Here is how to teach telling apart "b" and "d." The other letters will be discussed later.

"b" and "d" Make Your Bed

If your child cannot remember if it's "b" or "d", they can make their hands into a bed. Tell them to make their left-hand into a "b" and their right-hand into a "d." The letter bellies will touch each other and they have made a "bed." They can then see which hand the print letter looks like to determine whether it is a "b" or a "d."

Some people do not want others to see them "making their bed." This technique can be done with hands resting in the lap. No one will notice what is happening, but the reader or speller will get the reminder they need.

Make your "bed" version 1

OR

Make your "bed" version 2

- Show your child this letter.
- Say the name of this letter.
- Have your child repeat the letter's name.
- Show your child how to trace the letter.
- Have your child trace the letter.

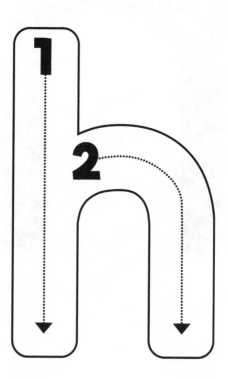

- Tell your child, "The name of this letter is 'h.' Its keyword is hat."
- Have your child repeat the keyword.
- Tell your child, "The letter 'h' says /h/ just like the beginning sound in hat."
- Touch your pointer finger to your thumb and say, /h./
- Have your child touch their pointer finger to their thumb and repeat the sound /h./
- Have your child trace or draw the letter in a fun, multisensory way.

When we write sentences or names, we start them with capital letters. This is what a capital 'H' looks like.

This is a Capital 'H' and a lowercase 'h' typed on a computer.

Hh

You may wish to show your child the Capital Letter Card from www.dogonalogbooks.com/printables.

This may look like a capital "I."
It is actually a lowercase "L."

- Show your child this letter.
- Say the name of this letter.
- Have your child repeat the letter's name.
- Show your child how to trace the letter.
- Have your child trace the letter.

- Tell your child, "The name of this letter is 'l.' Its keyword is lamp."
- Have your child repeat the keyword.
- Tell your child, "The letter 'l' says /l/ just like the beginning sound in lamp."
- Touch your pointer finger to your thumb and say, /l./
- Have your child touch their pointer finger to their thumb and repeat the sound /l./
- Have your child trace or draw the letter in a fun, multisensory way.

When we write sentences or names, we start them with capital letters. This is what a capital 'L' looks like.

L

This is a Capital 'L' and a lowercase 'l' typed on a computer.

Ll

You may wish to show your child the Capital Letter Card from www.dogonalogbooks.com/printables.

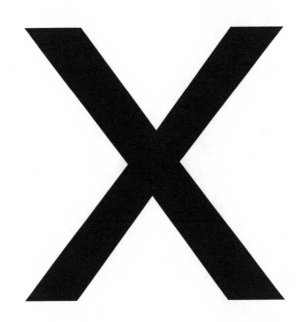

- Show your child this letter.
- Say the name of this letter.
- Have your child repeat the letter's name.
- Show your child how to trace the letter.
- Have your child trace the letter.

- Tell your child, "The name of this letter is 'x.' Its keyword is fox."
- Have your child repeat the keyword.
- Tell your child, "The letter 'x' says /ks/ just like the **ending** sound in fox. **Most keyword sounds are at the beginning of words. This time it the sound is at the end.**"
- Touch your pointer finger to your thumb and say, /ks./
- Have your child touch their pointer finger to their thumb and repeat the sound /ks./
- Have your child trace or draw the letter in a fun, multisensory way.

When we write sentences or names, we start them with capital letters. This is what a capital 'X' looks like.

This is a Capital 'X' and a lowercase 'x' typed on a computer.

You may wish to show your child the Capital Letter Card from www.dogonalogbooks.com/printables.

Blending Words

Ask your child to say each of these sounds while tapping their pointer finger to their thumb. Do not ask them to blend the sounds.

b

o

x

Now ask your child to place their fingers under each letter and say each sound.

Ask them to repeat this as quickly as they can until they say the word "box."

If they do not understand what you are asking them to do, demonstrate this then have them copy you.

Ask your child to say each of these sounds while tapping
their pointer finger to their thumb. Do not ask them to
blend the sounds.

l

o

t

Now ask your child to place their fingers under each letter and say each sound.

Ask them to repeat this as quickly as they can until they say the word "lot."

If they do not understand what you are asking them to do, demonstrate this then have them copy you.

lot

Review the lowercase and capital letters below. You may wish to keep the Capital Letter cards near your child so they can refer to them if they need to.

Bb, Hh, Ll, Xx

Reading Words

Have your child decode (sound out) these words. Some of these words are names. Names start with Capital Letters. Have your child tap and sound out these words. They can also be downloaded in a pdf bookfold, 8.5 x 11 sheet, or flashcards that can be used as gamecards with any of the DOG ON A LOG gameboards.

bag   bat   lab

hot   had   hat

lag   lad   fox

box   Max   Sal

Here are some silly words your child can sound out. Sounding out silly words is a good skill because it means they are not guessing.

bax   hab   lon

If you have a magnetic letter board, you and your child can play with the letters to make real or silly words. Take time to substitute one letter at a time so your child can see how you make new words by changing the letters. If you don't have a magnetic board, you can use the sound cards to create words.

Writing

It is important that your child practice writing along with practicing reading. They need multiple senses involved to cement these new skills. They also need to learn how to write.

Ask your child to write a few of the words from the prior page. You can download printable lined paper at www.dogonalogbooks.com/printables. To avoid using so much paper, you can also get a white board with guide lines and dry erase markers. Kids should still practice on paper as I have been told some don't always transfer their skills from the white board to paper. However, the white board is one more way to practice.

Time to Rhyme

Let's make rhymes by changing the first letter of the following words.

Read this word:

tab

Let's change the first letter to "c."

Read this word:

cab

Let's change the first letter to "f."

Read this word:

fab

You can use magnetic letter boards or sound cards to play this game. Create silly words or real words.

Switch the End

What happens if we change the last letter?

Read this word:

lag

Let's change the last letter to "d."

Read this word:

lad

Let's change the last letter to "b."

Read this word:

lab

You can use magnetic letter boards or sound cards to play this game. Create silly words or real words.

Sight Words for Sentences

Please help your child learn the following sight words. You can use the method on page 80 or a method of your choice.

does

go

of

Sentence Time

Have your child read the sentences on the next page. They should tap each sound. Make sure they tap the correct fingers.

First sound: Tap pointer finger to thumb.
Second sound: Tap middle finger to thumb.
Third sound: Tap ring finger to thumb.

If your child cannot remember a letter's sound, ask them the keyword. If that does not help them remember the sound, show them the keyword card or table.

It may be easier at first if you hide all the sentences below what your child is reading. You can do this by covering them with a piece of paper.

Pace yourself. If your child is struggling, just read a sentence or two. Congratulate them for their hard work (because this IS hard for them.) If your child is still able to proceed, trace the letters, play games finding objects that have the same beginning, ending, or middle letter. Come back to this when your child is ready.

If your child would prefer to read the sentences from a "book," they are available as downloadable printable bookfold pdfs at www.dogonalogbooks.com/printables. They can also be downloaded in list form on 8.5 x 11 paper.

1. Does Rob go to the lab?

2. Can Max fax the tax man?

3. Sal has to go to the cab.

4. The hog does not go to

the bog.

5. Max has a can of Tab.

6. Sal has a hot rod.

7. Can Rob nab the fox?

8. Sal has a fab hat box.

Story Time

If your child would prefer to read the story from a kid-friendly book, the stories are available in *Kids' Squiggles (Letters Make Words.)*

Max and Sal

Max and Sal ran to the cab.

The cab has a lot of gas.

The cab does not lag.

The cab can go and go and go.

The cab got to the bog.

The bog is hot.

The cab does go to the dam.

Max and Sal got to the dam.

The dam is not hot.

Max and Sal gab and gab at the dam.

Letter Group 5

i, p, k, j

Sight Words Introduced:
her, says

Vowel: i

Remind your child, "Every syllable has a vowel. We will get to meet the vowels one by one.

"The third vowel we will meet is…"

- Show your child this letter.
- Say the name of this letter.
- Have your child repeat the letter's name.
- Show your child how to trace the letter.
- Have your child trace the letter.

- Tell your child, "The name of this letter is 'i.' Its keyword is itch. You can also say, 'I itch.'" You may want to show them the keyword card and keyword table.
- Have your child repeat the keyword.
- Tell your child, "The letter 'i' says /i/ just like the beginning sound in itch."
- Touch your pointer finger to your thumb and say, /i./
- Have your child touch their pointer finger to their thumb and repeat the sound /i./
- Have your child trace or draw the letter in a fun, multisensory way.

When we write sentences or names, we start them with capital letters. This is what a capital 'I' looks like.

I

This is a Capital 'I' and a lowercase 'i' typed on a computer.

Ii

You may wish to show your child the Capital Letter Card from www.dogonalogbooks.com/printables.

- Show your child this letter.
- Say the name of this letter.
- Have your child repeat the letter's name.
- Show your child how to trace the letter.
- Have your child trace the letter.

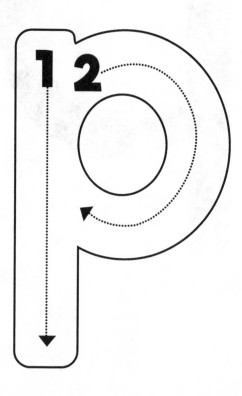

- Tell your child, "The name of this letter is 'p.' Its keyword is pan."
- Have your child repeat the keyword.
- Tell your child, "The letter 'p' says /p/ just like the beginning sound in pan."
- Touch your pointer finger to your thumb and say, /p./
- Have your child touch their pointer finger to their thumb and repeat the sound /p./
- Have your child trace or draw the letter in a fun, multisensory way.

When we write sentences or names, we start them with capital letters. This is what a capital 'P' looks like.

P

This is a Capital 'P' and a lowercase 'p' typed on a computer.

Pp

You may wish to show your child the Capital Letter Card from www.dogonalogbooks.com/printables.

Letter Reversals

Letter Reversals

Since lowercase "b" "d" "p" "g" and "q" can look alike to many people, you can help your child remember "p" and "g" this way.

"p" and "g"
See a Pig

If your child cannot remember if it's "p" or "g", they can make their hands into a pig. Tell them to make thumbs down and touch their fingers together. Their fingers will be the letter bellies. The letter bellies will touch each other and they will see a "pig." They can then see which hand the print letter looks like to determine whether it is a "p" or a "g."

Some people do not want others to see them "making a pig." This technique can be done with hands resting in the lap. No one will notice what is happening, but the reader or speller will get the reminder they need.

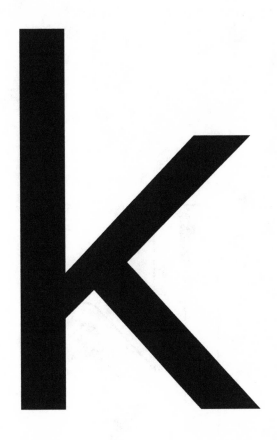

- Show your child this letter.
- Say the name of this letter.
- Have your child repeat the letter's name.
- Show your child how to trace the letter.
- Have your child trace the letter.

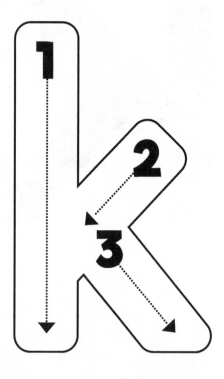

- Tell your child, "The name of this letter is 'k.' Its keyword is kite."
- Have your child repeat the keyword.
- Tell your child, "The letter 'k' says /k/ just like the beginning sound in kite."
- Touch your pointer finger to your thumb and say, /k./
- Have your child touch their pointer finger to their thumb and repeat the sound /k./
- Have your child trace or draw the letter in a fun, multisensory way.

When we write sentences or names, we start them with capital letters. This is what a capital 'K' looks like.

K

This is a Capital 'K' and a lowercase 'k' typed on a computer.

You may wish to show your child the Capital Letter Card from www.dogonalogbooks.com/printables.

- Show your child this letter.
- Say the name of this letter.
- Have your child repeat the letter's name.
- Show your child how to trace the letter.
- Have your child trace the letter.

- Tell your child, "The name of this letter is 'j.' Its keyword is jug."
- Have your child repeat the keyword.
- Tell your child, "The letter 'j' says /j/ just like the beginning sound in jug."
- Touch your pointer finger to your thumb and say, /j./
- Have your child touch their pointer finger to their thumb and repeat the sound /j./
- Have your child trace or draw the letter in a fun, multisensory way.

When we write sentences or names, we start them with capital letters. This is what a capital 'J' looks like.

J

This is a Capital 'J' and a lowercase 'j' typed on a computer.

Jj

You may wish to show your child the Capital Letter Card from www.dogonalogbooks.com/printables.

Blending Words

Ask your child to say each of these sounds while tapping their pointer finger to their thumb. Do not ask them to blend the sounds.

p

i

g

Now ask your child to place their fingers under each letter and say each sound.

Ask them to repeat this as quickly as they can until they say the word "pig."

If they do not understand what you are asking them to do, demonstrate this then have them copy you.

Ask your child to say each of these sounds while tapping their pointer finger to their thumb. Do not ask them to blend the sounds.

k

i

t

Now ask your child to place their fingers under each letter and say each sound.

Ask them to repeat this as quickly as they can until they say the word "kit."

If they do not understand what you are asking them to do, demonstrate this then have them copy you.

Review the lowercase and Capital letters below. You may wish to keep the Capital Letter cards near your child so they can refer to them if they need to.

Ii, Pp, Kk, Jj

Reading Words

Have your child decode (sound out) these words. Some of these words are names. Names start with Capital Letters. Have your child tap and sound out these words. They can also be downloaded in a pdf bookfold, 8.5 x 11 sheet, or flashcards that can be used as gamecards with any of the DOG ON A LOG gameboards.

pig	pit	pin
kit	kin	kid
jig	jam	tip
Kim	Jan	Jim

Here are some silly words your child can sound out. Sounding out silly words is a good skill because it means they are not guessing.

jat	kom	pob

If you have a magnetic letter board, you and your child can play with the letters to make real or silly words. Take time to substitute one letter at a time so your child can see how you make new words by changing the letters. If you don't have a magnetic board, you can use the sound cards to create words.

Writing

It is important that your child practice writing along with practicing reading. They need multiple senses involved to cement these new skills. They also need to learn how to write.

Ask your child to write a few of the words from the prior page. You can download printable lined paper at www.dogonalogbooks.com/printables. To avoid using so much paper, you can also get a white board with guide lines and dry erase markers. Kids should still practice on paper as I have been told some don't always transfer their skills from the white board to paper. However, the white board is one more way to practice.

Time to Rhyme

Let's make rhymes by changing the first letter of the following words.

Read this word:

Kim

Let's change the first letter to "J."

Read this word:

Jim

Let's change the first letter to "T."

Read this word:

Tim

You can use magnetic letter boards or sound cards to play this game. Create silly words or real words.

Switch the End

What happens if we change the last letter?

Read this word:

pig

Let's change the last letter to "t."

Read this word:

pit

Let's change the last letter to "n."

Read this word:

pin

You can use magnetic letter boards or sound cards to play this game. Create silly words or real words.

Change the Middle

What happens if we change the middle letter?

Read this word:

pit

Let's change the middle letter to "o."

Read this word:

pot

Let's try another word. Read this word:

lip

Let's change the middle letter to "a."

Read this word:

lap

You can use magnetic letter boards or sound cards to play this game. Create silly words or real words.

Sight Words for Sentences

Please help your child learn the following sight words. You can use the method on page 80 or a method of your choice.

her

says

Sentence Time

Have your child read the sentences on the next page. They should tap each sound. Make sure they tap the correct fingers.

First sound: Tap pointer finger to thumb.
Second sound: Tap middle finger to thumb.
Third sound: Tap ring finger to thumb.

If your child cannot remember a letter's sound, ask them the keyword. If that does not help them remember the sound, show them the keyword card or table.

It may be easier at first if you hide all the sentences below what your child is reading. You can do this by covering them with a piece of paper.

Pace yourself. If your child is struggling, just read a sentence or two. Congratulate them for their hard work (because this IS hard for them.) If your child is still able to proceed, trace the letters, play games finding objects that have the same beginning, ending, or middle letter. Come back to this when your child is ready.

If your child would prefer to read the sentences from a "book," they are available as downloadable printable bookfold pdfs at www.dogonalogbooks.com/printables. They can also be downloaded in list form on 8.5 x 11 paper.

1.The pig has a bit of hog mix.

2.Kim does dig a pit.

3.Jim says, "Does her hot rod go?"

4.The tip of the mop got a rip.

5.Sid got rid of the can of pop.

6."Hop in the cab," Kim says to her kid.

7.Pam got the big top to fit.

8.The bib has a six on it.

Story Time

If your child would prefer to read the story from a kid-friendly book, the stories are available in *Kids' Squiggles (Letters Make Words.)*

Bip, Sop, Lob

Jan has a lid.

Jan does tap the lid.

The lid says, "Bip, bop, dop."

Jan has a sis.

Her sis has a pan.

Sis does tap the pan.

The pan says, "Sop, sop, sop."

Mom has a mop.

Mom does tap the mop on the mat.

The mop says, "Lip, dop, lop."

Dad does sit on the mat.

Dad does nod to the tap, tap, tap.

Dad does nod to the, "Bip, sop, lop."

Letter Group 6

u, y, z, qu

Vowel: u

Remind your child, "Every syllable has a vowel. We will get to meet the vowels one by one.

"The fourth vowel we will meet is…"

- Show your child this letter.
- Say the name of this letter.
- Have your child repeat the letter's name.
- Show your child how to trace the letter.
- Have your child trace the letter.

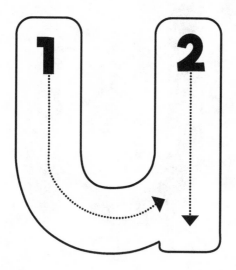

- Tell your child, "The name of this letter is 'u.' Its keyword is up.'" You may want to show them the keyword card and keyword table.
- Have your child repeat the keyword.
- Tell your child, "The letter 'u' says /u/ just like the beginning sound in up."
- Touch your pointer finger to your thumb and say, /u./
- Have your child touch their pointer finger to their thumb and repeat the sound /u./
- Have your child trace or draw the letter in a fun, multisensory way.

When we write sentences or names, we start them with capital letters. This is what a capital 'U' looks like.

U

This is a Capital 'U' and a lowercase 'u' typed on a computer.

Uu

You may wish to show your child the Capital Letter Card from www.dogonalogbooks.com/printables.

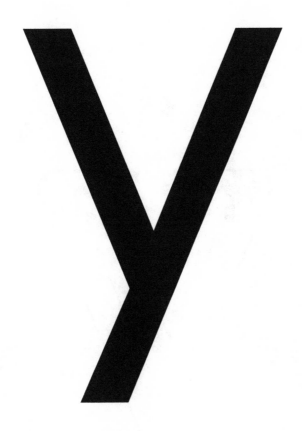

- Show your child this letter.
- Say the name of this letter.
- Have your child repeat the letter's name.
- Show your child how to trace the letter.
- Have your child trace the letter.

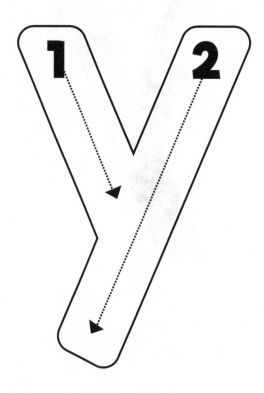

- Tell your child, "The name of this letter is 'y.' Its keyword is yellow.'" You may want to show them the keyword card and keyword table.
- Have your child repeat the keyword.
- Tell your child, "The letter 'y' says /y/ just like the beginning sound in yellow."
- Touch your pointer finger to your thumb and say, /y./
- Have your child touch their pointer finger to their thumb and repeat the sound /y./
- Have your child trace or draw the letter in a fun, multisensory way.

When we write sentences or names, we start them with capital letters. This is what a capital 'Y' looks like.

This is a Capital 'Y' and a lowercase 'y' typed on a computer.

You may wish to show your child the Capital Letter Card from www.dogonalogbooks.com/printables.

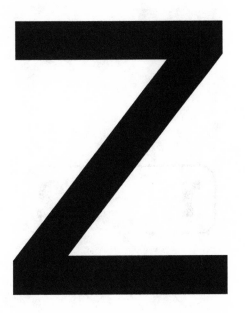

- Show your child this letter.
- Say the name of this letter.
- Have your child repeat the letter's name.
- Show your child how to trace the letter.
- Have your child trace the letter.

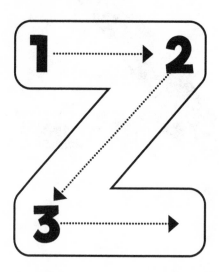

- Tell your child, "The name of this letter is 'z.' Its keyword is zebra.'" You may want to show them the keyword card and keyword table.
- Have your child repeat the keyword.
- Tell your child, "The letter 'z' says /z/ just like the beginning sound in zebra."
- Touch your pointer finger to your thumb and say, /z./
- Have your child touch their pointer finger to their thumb and repeat the sound /z./
- Have your child trace or draw the letter in a fun, multisensory way.

When we write sentences or names, we start them with capital letters. This is what a capital 'Z' looks like.

Z

This is a Capital 'Z' and a lowercase 'z' typed on a computer.

Zz

You may wish to show your child the Capital Letter Card from www.dogonalogbooks.com/printables.

qu

- Show your child this letter.
- Say the name of this letter.
- Have your child repeat the letter's name.
- Show your child how to trace the letter.
- Have your child trace the letter.

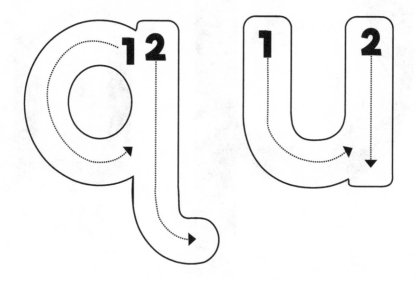

- Tell your child, "The name of this letter is 'q.' Its keyword is queen. **'Q' is a chicken letter. It is scared so it always goes with its buddy 'u.' We always write 'qu' together."** You may want to show them the keyword card and keyword table.
- Have your child repeat the keyword.
- Tell your child, "The letters 'qu' say /kw/ just like the beginning sound in queen."
- Touch your pointer finger to your thumb and say, /kw./
- Have your child touch their pointer finger to their thumb and repeat the sound /kw./
- Have your child trace or draw the letter in a fun, multisensory way.

When we write sentences or names, we start them with capital letters. This is what a capital 'Q' looks like with its buddy 'u.'

Qu

This is a Capital 'Q' and a lowercase 'q' typed on a computer. They always have their buddy 'u."

Qu qu

You may wish to show your child the Capital Letter Card from www.dogonalogbooks.com/printables.

Letter Reversals

Since lowercase "b" "d" "p" "g" and "q" can look alike to many people, you can help your child think of "q" this way.

"q"
Is a Chicken Letter

If your child cannot remember if it's "q" or some other letter, tell them to look and see if its buddy "u" is there. There may be times when "p" or "g" have a "u" with it, but if there is no "u" they will know it is not a "q."

Blending Words

Ask your child to say each of these sounds while tapping their pointer finger to their thumb. Do not ask them to blend the sounds.

qu

i

z

Now ask your child to place their fingers under each letter and say each sound.

Ask them to repeat this as quickly as they can until they say the word "quiz."

If they do not understand what you are asking them to do, demonstrate this then have them copy you.

quiz

Ask your child to say each of these sounds while tapping their pointer finger to their thumb. Do not ask them to blend the sounds.

y

u

m

Now ask your child to place their fingers under each letter and say each sound.

Ask them to repeat this as quickly as they can until they say the word "yum."

If they do not understand what you are asking them to do, demonstrate this then have them copy you.

Review the lowercase and capital letters below. You may wish to keep the Capital Letter cards near your child so they can refer to them if they need to.

Uu, Yy, Zz, Qu qu

Reading Words

Have your child decode (sound out) these words. Some of these words are names. Names start with Capital Letters. Have your child tap and sound out these words. They can also be downloaded in a pdf bookfold, 8.5 x 11 sheet, or flashcards that can be used as gamecards with any of the DOG ON A LOG gameboards.

quit	quip	yum
yam	yap	zap
bus	cup	gum
rug	fun	Quin

Here are some silly words your child can sound out. Sounding out silly words is a good skill because it means they are not guessing.

zug	yut	quam

If you have a magnetic letter board, you and your child can play with the letters to make real or silly words. Take time to substitute one letter at a time so your child can see how you make new words by changing the letters. If you don't have a magnetic board, you can use the sound cards to create words.

Writing

It is important that your child practice writing along with practicing reading. They need multiple senses involved to cement these new skills. They also need to learn how to write.

Ask your child to write a few of the words from the prior page. You can download printable lined paper at www.dogonalogbooks.com/printables. To avoid using so much paper, you can also get a white board with guide lines and dry erase markers. Kids should still practice on paper as I have been told some don't always transfer their skills from the white board to paper. However, the white board is one more way to practice.

Time to Rhyme

Let's make rhymes by changing the first letter of the following words.

Read this word:

run

Let's change the first letter to "b."

Read this word:

bun

Let's change the first letter to "s."

Read this word:

sun

You can use magnetic letter boards or sound cards to play this game. Create silly words or real words.

Switch the End

What happens if we change the last letter?

Read this word:

zap

Let's change the last letter to "g."

Read this word:

zag

Let's change the last letter to "m."

Read this silly word:

zam

You can use magnetic letter boards or sound cards to play this game. Create silly words or real words.

Change the Middle

What happens if we change the middle letter?

Read this word:

yup

Let's change the middle letter to "i."

Read this word:

yip

Let's try another word. Read this silly word:

zum

Let's change the middle letter to "a."

Read this silly word:

zam

You can use magnetic letter boards or sound cards to play this game. Create silly words or real words.

Sentence Time

Have your child read the sentences on the next page. They should tap each sound. Make sure they tap the correct fingers.

First sound: Tap pointer finger to thumb.
Second sound: Tap middle finger to thumb.
Third sound: Tap ring finger to thumb.

If your child cannot remember a letter's sound, ask them the keyword. If that does not help them remember the sound, show them the keyword card or table.

It may be easier at first if you hide all the sentences below what your child is reading. You can do this by covering them with a piece of paper.

Pace yourself. If your child is struggling, just read a sentence or two. Congratulate them for their hard work (because this IS hard for them.) If your child is still able to proceed, trace the letters, play games finding objects that have the same beginning, ending, or middle letter. Come back to this when your child is ready.

If your child would prefer to read the sentences from a "book," they are available as downloadable printable bookfold pdfs at www.dogonalogbooks.com/printables. They can also be downloaded in list form on 8.5 x 11 paper.

1. Tup dug in the mud and got a big bug.

2. Gus had nut and yam on a bun. It was yum.

3. Quin got to hop and run.

4. Let us go get a bit of gum.

5. The hot rod says, "Zip, zap, zip."

6. Quin got to hug the pug dog.

7. Jim has a sub in the tub.

8. Gus got gum on the big rug.

Story Time

If your child would prefer to read the story from a kid-friendly book, the stories are available in *Kids' Squiggles (Letters Make Words.)*

Jan and Quin

Jan has a pal.
Her pal is Quin.
Quin has a pup.
The pup is his pal.
The pup says, "Yap, yap."
Jan has a dog.
Her dog is Tup.
Tup says, "Yip, yip."
Jan says to Quin, "Let us go for a run."
Jan and Tup run zig.
Quin and his pup run zag.
Jan and Quin zig and zag and run, run, run.

Letter Group 7

e, v, w

Vowel: e

Remind your child, "Every syllable has a vowel. We will get to meet the vowels one by one.

"The fifth vowel we will meet is..."

- Show your child this letter.
- Say the name of this letter.
- Have your child repeat the letter's name.
- Show your child how to trace the letter.
- Have your child trace the letter.

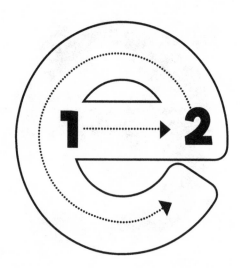

- Tell your child, "The name of this letter is 'e.' Its keyword is Ed.'" You may want to show them the keyword card and keyword table.
- Have your child repeat the keyword.
- Tell your child, "The letter 'e' says /e/ just like the beginning sound in Ed."
- Touch your pointer finger to your thumb and say, /e./
- Have your child touch their pointer finger to their thumb and repeat the sound /e./
- Have your child trace or draw the letter in a fun, multisensory way.

When we write sentences or names, we start them with capital letters. This is what a capital 'E' looks like.

E

This is a Capital 'E' and a lowercase 'e' typed on a computer.

Ee

You may wish to show your child the Capital Letter Card from www.dogonalogbooks.com/printables.

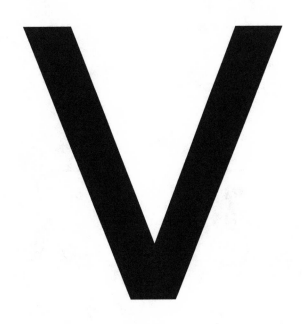

- Show your child this letter.
- Say the name of this letter.
- Have your child repeat the letter's name.
- Show your child how to trace the letter.
- Have your child trace the letter.

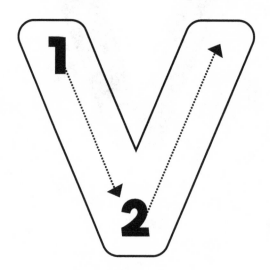

- Tell your child, "The name of this letter is 'v.' Its keyword is van.'" You may want to show them the keyword card and keyword table.
- Have your child repeat the keyword.
- Tell your child, "The letter 'v' says /v/ just like the beginning sound in van."
- Touch your pointer finger to your thumb and say, /v./
- Have your child touch their pointer finger to their thumb and repeat the sound /v./
- Have your child trace or draw the letter in a fun, multisensory way.

When we write sentences or names, we start them with capital letters. This is what a capital 'V' looks like.

This is a Capital 'V' and a lowercase 'v' typed on a computer.

You may wish to show your child the Capital Letter Card from www.dogonalogbooks.com/printables.

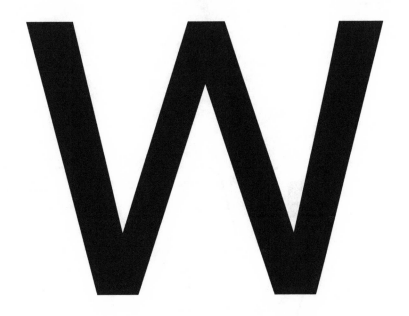

- Show your child this letter.
- Say the name of this letter.
- Have your child repeat the letter's name.
- Show your child how to trace the letter.
- Have your child trace the letter.

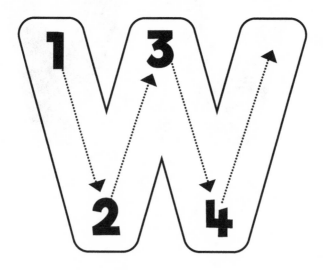

- Tell your child, "The name of this letter is 'w.' Its keyword is wind.'" You may want to show them the keyword card and keyword table.
- Have your child repeat the keyword.
- Tell your child, "The letter 'w' says /w/ just like the beginning sound in wind."
- Touch your pointer finger to your thumb and say, /w./
- Have your child touch their pointer finger to their thumb and repeat the sound /w./
- Have your child trace or draw the letter in a fun, multisensory way.

When we write sentences or names, we start them with capital letters. This is what a capital 'W' looks like.

This is a Capital 'W' and a lowercase 'w' typed on a computer.

You may wish to show your child the Capital Letter Card from www.dogonalogbooks.com/printables.

Review the lowercase and capital letters below. You may wish to keep the Capital Letter cards near your child so they can refer to them if they need to.

Ee, Vv, Ww

Reading Words

Have your child decode (sound out) these words. Some of these words are names. Names start with Capital Letters. Have your child tap and sound out these words. They can also be downloaded in a pdf bookfold, 8.5 x 11 sheet, or flashcards that can be used as gamecards with any of the DOG ON A LOG gameboards.

web	wet	wed
vet	vat	van
wag	win	wax
wig	Bev	Val

Here are some silly words your child can sound out. Sounding out silly words is a good skill because it means they are not guessing.

vog	wex	wid

If you have a magnetic letter board, you and your child can play with the letters to make real or silly words. Take time to substitute one letter at a time so your child can see how you make new words by changing the letters. If you don't have a magnetic board, you can use the sound cards to create words.

Writing

It is important that your child practice writing along with practicing reading. They need multiple senses involved to cement these new skills. They also need to learn how to write.

Ask your child to write a few of the words from the prior page. You can download printable lined paper at www.dogonalogbooks.com/printables. To avoid using so much paper, you can also get a white board with guide lines and dry erase markers. Kids should still practice on paper as I have been told some don't always transfer their skills from the white board to paper. However, the white board is one more way to practice.

Time to Rhyme

Let's make rhymes by changing the first letter of the following words.

Read this word:

wet

Let's change the first letter to "v."

Read this word:

vet

Let's change the first letter to "s."

Read this word:

set

You can use magnetic letter boards or sound cards to play this game. Create silly words or real words.

Switch the End

What happens if we change the last letter?

Read this word:

win

Let's change the last letter to "g."

Read this word:

wig

Let's change the last letter to "t."

Read this word:

wit

You can use magnetic letter boards or sound cards to play this game. Create silly words or real words.

Change the Middle

What happens if we change the middle letter?

Read this word:

vet

Let's change the middle letter to "a."

Read this word:

vat

Let's try another word. Read this word:

wet

Let's change the middle letter to "i."

Read this word:

wit

You can use magnetic letter boards or sound cards to play this game. Create silly words or real words.

Sentence Time

Have your child read the sentences on the next page. They should tap each sound. Make sure they tap the correct fingers.

First sound: Tap pointer finger to thumb.
Second sound: Tap middle finger to thumb.
Third sound: Tap ring finger to thumb.

If your child cannot remember a letter's sound, ask them the keyword. If that does not help them remember the sound, show them the keyword card or table.

It may be easier at first if you hide all the sentences below what your child is reading. You can do this by covering them with a piece of paper.

Pace yourself. If your child is struggling, just read a sentence or two. Congratulate them for their hard work (because this IS hard for them.) If your child is still able to proceed, trace the letters, play games finding objects that have the same beginning, ending, or middle letter. Come back to this when your child is ready.

If your child would prefer to read the sentences from a "book," they are available as downloadable printable bookfold pdfs at www.dogonalogbooks.com/printables. They can also be downloaded in list form on 8.5 x 11 paper.

1. Bev got in the van and got her cat to the vet.

2. A bug is in her wig.

3. The vat of wax is hot.

4. Tup ran to get in the van.

5. Did Tam the cat get wet?

6. Sal and Sid wed at sun set.

7. Bev does not quit the quiz.

8. The vet does hug her pet ram.

Story Time

If your child would prefer to read the story from a kid-friendly book, the stories are available in *Kids' Squiggles (Letters Make Words.)*

Wet Van

Jan and Quin are wet.
Jan and her dad are wet.
Dad and the van are wet.
Jan has a rag. A wet rag. Jan does rub the wet rag on the van.
Quin has mop. A wet mop. Quin does rub the wet mop on the van.
Dad has a wet rag. Dad does rub the top of the van.
Dad has a rag. It is not wet. He does rub the van. The van is not wet.

CONGRATULATIONS!!!

You did it. You broke The Squiggle Code. You are on the Reading Pathway.

You should celebrate.

You could go for a walk or drive and look for letters, or even words, you recognize.

You can make a banner that says, "(Your child's name) DID IT!"

You can make a blue ribbon and tape it where you can see it.

Or...I bet you can figure out the best way you want to celebrate.

What's Next?

If your child is able to decode all the sounds presented in this book and read the types of words presented here, they are probably ready to move on to longer books and stories and phonics rules. Remember, they may still struggle or forget what they have learned. You will have to keep practicing and re-practicing the skills you thought they already knew. (Remember: repetition, repetition, repetition.) If they don't seem to cement these skills, you may want to find help as described on page 15.

Your child will do best with a systematic, sequential series of decodable books that slowly introduce new phonics rules. At this level, you can find a few decodable books with controlled sight words by a limited number of publishers. Unfortunately, the best ones I found were out of print and I had to search for used copies.

Most decodable books I found had just a few sentences. They are good because they build confidence while your child is practicing their new skills. Most kids aren't ready for longer books at the very beginning. The downside of these books is they are easily memorized. Once it is clear your child has memorized the book, it is time to move on as they aren't actually reading that particular book any more.

When you are ready for longer books and more complicated stories, there are very few options available. As I write this, your search for decodable chapter books will find just a handful of options. Even fewer will be written at the level that your child is ready for at this point on their path. This is why I started writing DOG ON A LOG Books; I could not find books for my eight-year-old when she was at this level.

DOG ON A LOG Books gradually add phonics rules. There are one to three new rules and a handful of new sight words at each Step. All books beyond the level of this book are available as chapter books. The first five Steps also have a companion series called Let's GO! Books. Although they tell the same stories as the chapter books, they have a lot less words so they aren't as intimidating for new readers. They are good bridge books to the chapter books. When your child has read the Let's GO! version, you can introduce the chapter book. "Look, it's the same story and same type of words you just read. Would you like to try it? It might be hard, but I know you can do it. We'll work together."

Most kids who read the Step 1 books are relieved they are not overly frustrated and they are incredibly proud of their accomplishment. When they get to Step 2, they will find the stories get more complicated and varied. (The addition of the suffix -s makes it easier to tell more nuanced stories.)

As the Steps continue, your child will find themselves meeting an expanding group of friends and neighbors in Tup and Jan's somewhat quirky world. In time they will even start reading series within the series including a five book mystery series that spans five Steps.

Writing DOG ON A LOG Books is one of the greatest fulfillments of my life. Knowing kids finally have a series of decodable books that helps them learn to read by taking small Steps forward brings me a type of happiness that is unmatched. I love reading reviews or emails about how proud a child was to have read an entire book. Please, share your child's story. That would make my day.

Tup says, "Ruff, ruff."

Happy Reading, Pamela Brookes

Capital Letters for Tracing

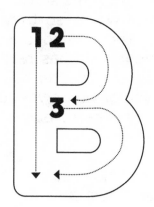

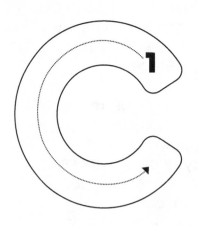

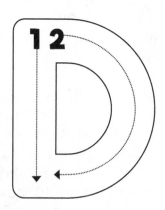

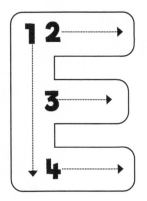

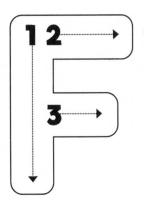

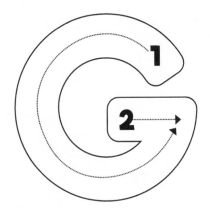

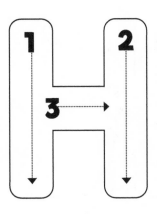

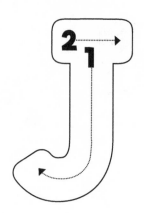

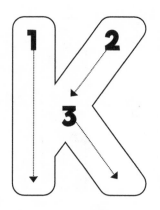

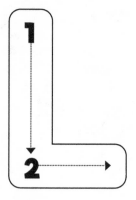

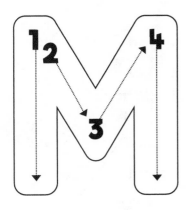

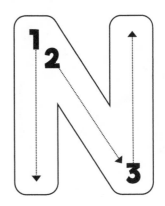

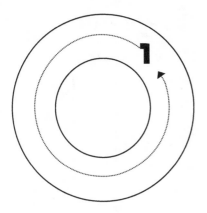

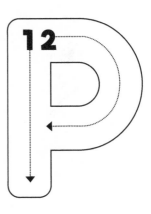

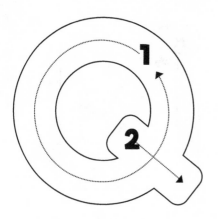

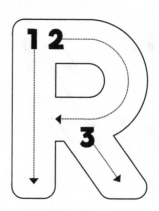

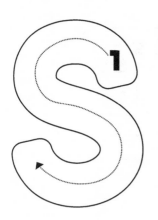

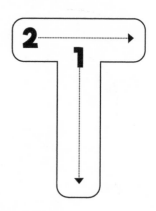

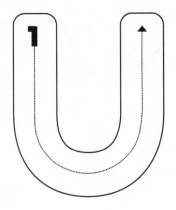

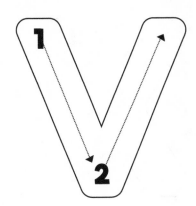

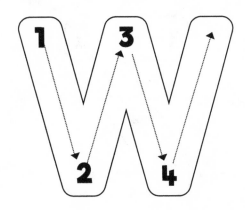

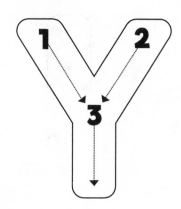

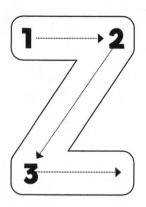

D'Nealian Letters
for Tracing

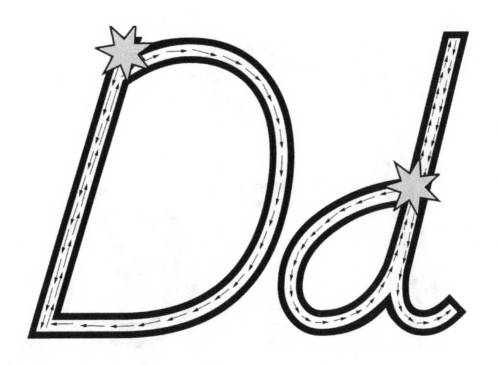

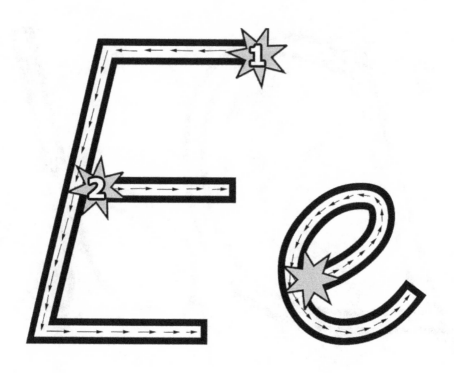

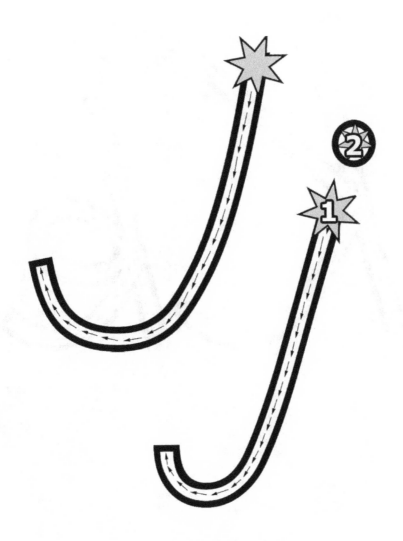

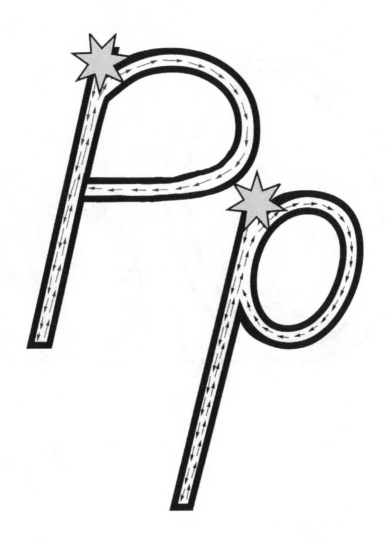

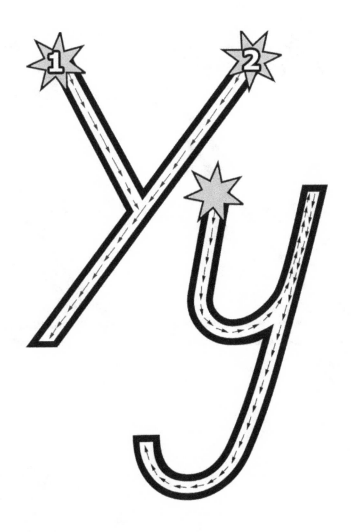

STRUGGLING READERS

Excerpts from
Teaching a Struggling Reader:
One Mom's Experience with Dyslexia

What if it's NOT Dyslexia

The Importance of
Early Intervention

(Links to the online resources are provided as endnotes.)

What If It's NOT Dyslexia

Sixty-five percent of fourth graders in the US are <u>not proficient at reading</u>.[i] Most of these children do not have dyslexia. I have spoken with numerous education professionals and read many articles including this one on <u>APM Reports</u>.[ii] The reason these children are not proficient with reading is usually because they are not taught reading with phonics. Their teachers were usually not taught how to teach phonics even though scientific research shows that systematic phonics is the best way for any student to learn to read.

The National Reading Panel reviewed 100,000 studies that examined reading instruction. They stated, "Systematic and explicit phonics instruction is more effective than non-systematic or no phonics instruction." In other words, the best way to learn to read is to be taught with a systematic phonics program. You can read their booklet <u>here</u>.[iii]

If your child is a struggling reader who has been taught with Whole Language or Balanced Literacy, you may want to approach their teacher, principal, or school board and asked them to review the scientific literature that says your child should be taught systematic explicit phonics. Then insist they teach all their students phonics in a scientifically proven manner. You may also consider using a program like <u>All About Reading</u>,[iv] <u>Explode the Code</u>,[v] or <u>MindPlay Virtual Reading Program</u>[vi] to teach them phonics yourself. Dr. Nancy Mather, a professor at the University of Arizona, has been very helpful to me and my books. You may want to check out the phonics program she co-authored: <u>Phonic Reading Lessons: Skills and Practice</u>.[vii]

My book, *The Squiggle Code (Letters Make Words,)* is a roadmap for teaching letter sounds, blending, and the beginning steps of reading. It is priced to be economical and there are numerous printable activities you can download from <u>www.dogonalogbooks.com/printables</u> that will supplement the material in the book.

A PBS partner, Education Week, produced this video, <u>Parents of Students With Dyslexia Have Transformed Reading Instruction</u>.[viii] It talks about how the advocacy of parents with children who have dyslexia has changed how all children in Arkansas are taught to read.

Here is basic information and an outline on the teaching of reading:

When teaching letter sounds, many parents and teachers demonstrate incorrect sounds. They may say, "B says buh and T says Tuh." Then they ask the child to read b-a-t. The child will say, "buh-a-tuh," instead of "bat." This <u>44 Phonemes video</u>[ix] will show you the correct way to make each of the 44 sounds in the (American) English language.

Although there can be more to it, the process of teaching reading with phonics is basically:

- Work on <u>segmenting and blending</u>.[x] There are many resources on <u>Pinterest</u>.[xi]

- Start by teaching the sounds of a few letters in a multi-sensory way. Draw them in shaving cream, trace them with your fingers, or any other fun way.

- After your student(s) have learned those letter sounds, sound out a few words with the letters they've been taught so far. Have your child put a finger under each letter and say the sounds as fast as they can until the child can say the whole word.

- Teach a few more letters.

- Sound out more words with those letters.

- Teach sight words, a few at a time. <u>Dolch words</u>[xii] are common sight words.

- Have the child read short decodable texts that provide practice with these letters and sounds.
- Move on to more individual phonics rules. Find a systematic decodable reading program. When they have mastered a set of phonics rules, move on to the next set of rules.

- Teach them about the six syllable types and how they may help determine the vowel sounds in words.

- Make sure to incorporate writing and reading the learned sounds/rules/sight words at each step of the way. Don't just focus on the rules, they need to practice reading and writing.

- My personal recommendation is to teach any learning reader to "tap" while sounding out. (See the earlier section on "tapping.") Some children may to try to guess at a word, but if they are tapping it really focuses them on the letters on the page so they will actually read it.

Here is a recommended order of teaching individual letter sounds. It is from *Phonic Reading Lessons* by Nancy Mather Ph.D., et al., 2007.

1. Vowel a: consonants s, m, f, t, n
2. No new vowel: consonants r, d, c, g
3. Vowel o; no new consonants
4. No new vowel; consonants b, h, l x
5. Vowel i; consonants p, k, j
6. Review of a, o, i, and 16 consonants
7. Vowel u; consonants y, z qu
8. Vowel e; consonants v, w
9. Review of u, e

The Importance of Early Intervention

The importance of early intervention cannot be stressed enough. Many teachers will tell parents, "Your child is just a late bloomer. They'll get it when they're ready. Let's just wait and watch." Although it is true that kids learn in different ways and at different rates, it seems individuals with dyslexia are pretty much born with different brains. The earlier they receive intervention, the better they may become at reading. <u>Tackling Dyslexia at an Early Age</u>[xiii] from Harvard Medical school states, "up to 70 percent of at-risk children who receive educational intervention in kindergarten or first grade become proficient readers." This article also talks about changes that occur in the brain with early school-age interventions.

On January 27, 2005, <u>Reading Rockets did an online chat with Dr. Sally Shaywitz,</u>[xiv] Dr, Shaywitz *(co-director of the <u>Yale Center for Dyslexia and Creativity</u>,[xv] at Yale University)* gave this list of signs seen in preschool children with dyslexia. If find it so important that I am including it in its entirety:

The most important clues in a preschool child are:

- *A family history of reading problems*
- *Delayed speech*
- *Lack of appreciation and enjoyment of rhymes e.g., not appreciating the rhymes in a Dr. Seuss book*
- *Not being able to recite rhymes by age 3*
- *Continuation of baby talk*
- *Trouble pronouncing words*
- *Trouble learning the alphabet (not the alphabet song, but knowing the individual names of the letters of the alphabet)*

It is important to keep in mind that you are looking for a pattern of these clues, ones that keeping occurring often. Not knowing a rhyme or the name of a letter once or twice is not what we are looking for. A pattern that occurs over and over again is what to look for.

A parent may be concerned their child could have dyslexia because of <u>red flags in their child's behavior</u>[xvi] or because of <u>family history</u>.[xvii] It seems to me that if a parent is concerned their child younger than 5 may have dyslexia, that taking actions at that early age could be highly beneficial. I have done multiple searches and contacted many dyslexia professionals asking for specific interventions to help preschool children who may have dyslexia. My online searches found no specific recommendations for how to help preschool children who may have dyslexia. Fortunately, I did receive very helpful information from two well-regarded Dyslexia Professionals.

Joanne Marttila Pierson, Ph.D., CCC-SLP, the Project Manager of <u>DyslexiaHelp</u>[xviii] at the University of Michigan stated, "Your best bet is to write about spoken language skills and development. As you know, spoken language undergirds learning to read, spell, and write, and so the better linguistic skills a child has, the better he is likely to do learning to read. For example, I have a <u>developmental milestone checker here</u>.[xix] As is suggested in this article, <u>Is Preschool Language Impairment a Risk Factor for Dyslexia in Adolescence?</u>,[xx] children with phonological disorders in preschool are at greater risk for reading disorder, which makes sense since the core deficit in dyslexia is in phonological processing (i.e., phonological awareness, phonological memory, rapid automatic naming.) And, books such as *Beyond Bedtime Stories* by Nell Duke are what you'd want to offer as resources."

As Dr. Pierson stated, many children with dyslexia have speech delays. Receiving Speech Therapy from a Speech Pathologist could make a tremendous difference when they start learning to read. (It will also be useful even if they do not have dyslexia.) When both of my children were babies, I frequently used the <u>Ages and Stages Questionnaires</u>^{xxi} just to make sure they were developing on target. When the results showed my daughter's speech was behind schedule, I got her evaluated. Because of this my daughter was able to start Speech Therapy at twelve months of age.

I'd always thought Speech Therapy was teaching children how to say words. Actually, articulation has been a very minor part of her therapy. It has focused more on helping her understand and express words. Speech Therapy helps children say, "I want the firetruck book." instead of "I want that." Early Intervention services are often free or very low cost for children from birth to three. Many school districts will continue with the (often free) services once the child turns three. You can learn more about <u>Early Intervention here</u>.^{xxii}

Reading to young children is perhaps one of the most important activities you can share. We read to our children multiple times a day during the early years. My daughter wanted to be read to even more than my son. She couldn't talk so she would scream if I didn't read to her for hours every day. I had the luxury of being a Stay-At-Home-Mom so we sat together reading book after book after book every day. I am not exaggerating when I say we read for hours each day for months, possibly years (those years are such a blur that I don't remember how long they lasted.) I now wonder if she craved being read to so much because she could not understand what language was and if being read to helped her try to figure it out. This article discusses <u>10 Benefits That Highlight the Importance of Reading with Young Children</u>.^{xxiii}

Another Dyslexia professional, Susan Barton of <u>Bright Solutions for Dyslexia</u>,[xxiv] also contacted me. She stated, "Most dyslexia professionals will not screen or test a child younger than age 5 1/2, plus the child must be at least halfway through kindergarten. But if you suspect dyslexia, I recommend you start doing the activities described in the following books now."

- *Phonemic Awareness in Young Children: A Classroom Curriculum* by Marilyn Adams Ph.D. and Barbara Foorman "Ph.D. M.A.T"

- *Preparing Children for Success in Reading: A Multisensory Guide for Teachers and Parents* by Nancy Sanders Royal based on the work of Beth Slingerland.

Since I could find no online links to share that explicitly said how to help preschool children who may have dyslexia, I searched for ways of teaching phonemic awareness in early childhood. Reading Rockets has a <u>list of specific activities</u>[xxv] that promote phonemic awareness. My favorite dyslexia website, <u>Homeschooling With Dyslexia</u>,[xxvi] has good phonemic awareness ideas. Pinterest is a great source for Phonemic Awareness. This link to <u>Pinterest</u>[xxvii] will offer you scads of ideas. I also searched for activities that would help any child gain skills to improve their reading abilities. There is an excellent list of suggestions at this article, <u>Help for Young Readers</u>.**[xxviii]**

As a parent, it can be really overwhelming to find and figure out exactly what skills are involved in phonological and phonemic awareness. As I was researching this, my eyes would sometimes roll back in my head from all the didactic information I found. Paragraph after paragraph of theory and information that was just so boring to read and didn't often tell me what activities were useful. I figured if I was overwhelmed trying to figure it all out, other parents might be at least as overwhelmed and frustrated. (I have the good fortune to have several dyslexia/reading/phonics experts that answer my questions, but many parents don't have that.)

This is why I have created this set of DOG ON A LOG Pup Books. I made them a Parent-Friendly Roadmap that show which skills kids need to learn and in which order. Because it is important that activities are personalized for each child, I include resources for where other activities can be found for free or low-cost. To make the search simpler for families, I have created boardgames and other activities that can be downloaded from my website.[xxix] There are activities for each section of *The Squiggle Code Books*. You do not need to read the books to use the activities. If you use the printable activities in order, you will be working on all the phonological and phonemic awareness skills.

My daughter and I have played the boardgames as a way to practice her sight words. In the homeschool co-op phonics class I taught, we played the same boardgames to practice rhyming, beginning/ending/middle sounds, and so much more. The boardgames can be adapted to any child's needs simply by switching out the game cards.

Please note. Although playing games and doing activities such as making up fun rhymes, counting syllables, and changing some of the sounds in words can be fun and advantageous for preschool children, I am not advocating teaching very young children to read. Children should not be forced to read before they are developmentally ready. One of my favorite books *Einstein Never Used Flashcards: How Our Children Really Learn-- And Why They Need to Play More and Memorize Less* by Kathy Hirsh-Pasek discusses multiple studies that show that children in play-based preschools ultimately do better than children in academic-based preschools. This pdf[xxx] also discusses the potential downsides of introducing reading at too young of an age.

Writing this section on Early Intervention brought out some of my Mom-Guilt. The *Help for Young Readers* article suggests rhyming activities with young children. We did lots of that with our son when he was a toddler and preschooler. It was so much fun. Then we tried it with our daughter. It wasn't so much fun. She didn't get it. No matter how many playful rhymes we made with her name or what we were saying and no matter how many rhyming books we read, she never understood rhyming. We eventually stopped trying. (She would learn to rhyme after multiple sessions with two different Orton-Gillingham teachers.) My guilty side wonders if we had kept trying to teach her rhyming and had done more phonemic awareness activities if it would have helped her when it was time to learn to read. We didn't know rhyming challenges could be a sign of dyslexia so we just stopped doing it and moved on to other ways to have fun with her.

We did so many good things for our daughter (we still do,) but I so regret we didn't do more phonemic awareness activities. I say this because, now that I know what activities we could have done, I think how hard parenting can be. For Stay-Home parents, not getting a break tires you out so much. For working parents there just aren't enough hours in a day. Every parent wants to do what is best for their child and sometimes (or often) life gets in the way. Please know that if you're feeling guilty that you can't do it all, you're not the only one that feels that way. Also know that every little action you take will make a difference in the long run. My husband likes to say, "Wrigley Gum made their fortune selling 5 cent packs of gum." (Ironically, William Wrigley Jr. of the chewing gum company had dyslexia.) Our daughter benefited from every book we read her and every Speech Therapy session she attended, even the ones where she refused to cooperate for half the session.

Keywords

Alphabet

Aa	Bb
apple	bat
Cc	Dd
cat	dog

Ee	Ff
Ed	fun
Gg	Hh
game	hat
Ii	Jj
itch	jug

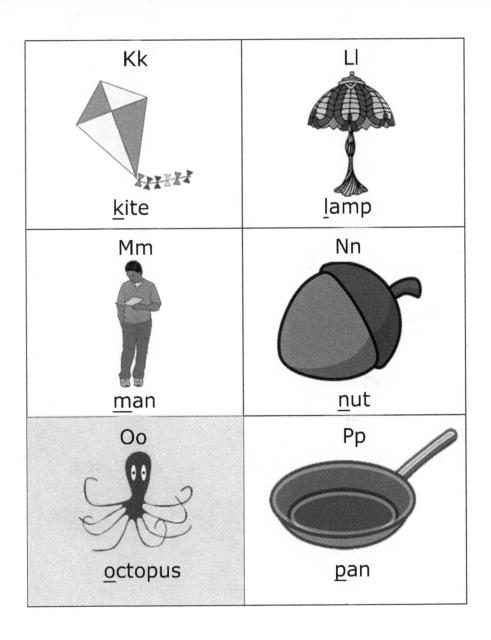

Kk	Ll
kite	lamp
Mm	Nn
man	nut
Oo	Pp
octopus	pan

Qu qu	Rr
queen	rat
Ss	Tt
snake	top
Uu	Vv
up	van

Ww	Xx
<u>w</u>ind	fo<u>x</u>
Yy	Zz
<u>y</u>ellow	<u>z</u>ebra

Phonics Progression

DOG ON A LOG Pup Books

Book 1
Phonological/Phonemic Awareness:
- Words
- Rhyming
- Syllables, identification, blending, segmenting
- Identifying individual letter sounds

Books 2-3
Phonemic Awareness/Phonics
- Consonants, primary sounds
- Short vowels
- Blending
- Introduction to sight words

DOG ON A LOG Let's GO! and Chapter Books

Step 1
- Consonants, primary sounds
- Short vowels
- Digraphs: ch, sh, th, wh, ck
- 2 and 3 sound words
- Possessive 's
-

Step 2
- Bonus letters (f, l, s, z after short vowel)
- "all"
- –s suffix

Step 3
- Letter Buddies: ang, ing, ong, ung, ank, ink, onk, unk

Step 4
- Consonant blends to make 4 sound words
- 3 and 4 sound words ending in –lk, -sk

Step 5
- Digraph blend –nch to make 3 and 4 sound words
- Silent e, including "-ke"

Step 6
- Exception words containing: ild, old, olt, ind, ost

Step 7
- 5 sounds in a closed syllable word plus suffix -s (crunch, slumps)
- 3 letter blends and up to 6 sounds in a closed syllable word (script, spring)

Step 8
- Two-syllable words with 2 closed syllables, not blends (sunset, chicken, unlock)

Step 9
- Two-syllable words with all previously introduced sounds including blends, exception words, and silent "e" (blacksmith, kindness, inside)
- Vowel digraphs: ai, ay, ea, ee, ie, oa, oe (rain, play, beach, tree, pie, boat, toe)

WATCH FOR MORE STEPS COMING SOON

Sight Word Progression

DOG ON A LOG Pup Books
a, does, go, has, her is, of, says, the, to

DOG ON A LOG Let's GO! and
Chapter Books

Step 1
a, and, are, be, does, go, goes, has, he, her, his, into, is, like, my, of, OK, says, see, she, the, they, to, want, you

Step 2
could, do, eggs, for, from, have, here, I, likes, me, nest, onto, or, puts, said, say, sees, should, wants, was, we, what, would, your

Step 3
as, Mr., Mrs., no, put, their, there, where

Step 4
push, saw

Step 5
come, comes, egg, pull, pulls, talk, walk, walks

Step 6
Ms., so, some, talks

Step 7
Hmmm, our, out, Pop E., TV

Step 8
Dr., friend, full, hi, island, people, please

Step 9
about, aunt, cousin, cousins, down, friends, hi, inn, know, knows, me, one, ones, TVs, two, water, welcome

More DOG ON A LOG Books

Most books available in Paperback, Hardback, and e-book formats

DOG ON A LOG Parent and Teacher Guides

Book 1 (Also in FREE e-book and PDF Bookfold)
- Teaching a Struggling Reader: One Mom's Experience with Dyslexia

Book 2 (FREE e-book and PDF Bookfold only)
- How to Use Decodable Books to Teach Reading

DOG ON A LOG Pup Books
Book 1
- Before the Squiggle Code (A Roadmap to Reading)

Books 2-3
- The Squiggle Code (Letters Make Words)
- Kids' Squiggles (Letters Make Words)

Let's GO! Books
have less text

Chapter Books
are longer

DOG ON A LOG Let's GO! and Chapter Books

Step 1
- The Dog on the Log
- The Pig Hat
- Chad the Cat
- Zip the Bug
- The Fish and the Pig

Step 2
- Mud on the Path
- The Red Hen
- The Hat and Bug Shop
- Babs the 'Bot
- The Cub

Step 3
- Mr. Bing has Hen Dots
- The Junk Lot Cat
- Bonk Punk Hot Rod
- The Ship with Wings
- The Sub in the Fish Tank

Step 4
- The Push Truck
- The Sand Hill
- Lil Tilt and Mr. Ling
- Musk Ox in the Tub
- The Trip to the Pond

Step 5
- Bake a Cake
- The Crane at the Cave
- Ride a Bike
- Crane or Crane?
- The Swing Gate

Step 6
- The Colt
- The Gold Bolt
- Hide in the Blinds
- The Stone Child
- Tolt the Kind Cat

Step 7
- Quest for A Grump Grunt
- The Blimp
- The Spring in the Lane
- Stamp for a Note
- Stripes and Splats

Step 8
- Anvil and Magnet
- The Mascot
- Kevin's Rabbit Hole
- The Humbug Vet and Medic Shop
- Chickens in the Attic

Step 9
- Trip to Cactus Gulch 1: The Step-Up Team
- Trip to Cactus Gulch 2: Into the Mineshaft
- Play the Bagpipes
- The Hidden Tale 1: The Lost Snapshot

All chapter books can be purchased individually or with all the same-step books in one volume.

Steps 1-5 can be bought as Let's GO! Books which are less text companions to the chapter books.

All titles can be bought as chapter books.

WATCH FOR MORE BOOKS COMING SOON

How You Can Help

Parents often worry that their child (or even adult learner) is not going to learn to read. Hearing other people's successes (especially when they struggled) can give worried parents or teachers hope. I would encourage others to share their experiences with products you've used by posting reviews at your favorite bookseller(s) stating how your child benefitted from those books or materials (whether it was DOG ON A LOG Books or another book or product.) This will help other parents and teachers know which products they should consider using. More than that, hearing your successes could truly help another family feel hopeful. It's amazing that something as seemingly small as a review can ease someone's concerns.

DOG ON A LOG
Quick Assessment

Have your child read the following words. If they can't read every word in a Step, that is probably where in the series they should start. Some children may benefit starting at an earlier step to help them build confidence in their reading abilities.

Get a printable assessment sheet at:
www.dogonalogbooks.com/how-to-use/
assessment-tool/

Step 1
fin, mash, sock, sub, cat, that, Dan's

Step 2
less, bats, tell, mall, chips, whiff, falls

Step 3
bangs, dank, honk, pings, chunk, sink, gong, rungs

Step 4
silk, fluff, smash, krill, drop, slim, whisk

Step 5
hunch, crate, rake, tote, inch, mote, lime

Step 6
child, molts, fold, hind, jolt, post, colds

Step 7
strive, scrape, splint, twists, crunch, prints, blend

Step 8
finish, denim, within, bathtub, sunset, medic, habit

Step 9
hundred, goldfinch, free, wheat, inhale, play, Joe

Step 10
be, remake, spry, repeat, silo, sometime, pinwheel

WATCH FOR MORE STEPS COMING SOON

Appreciation

There are a lot of behind the scenes people who help me with DOG ON A LOG Books. I cannot fully tell you how much I appreciate all they do.

Before the Squiggle Code and *The Squiggle Code* could not exist without the help from Dr. Nancy Mather of the University of Arizona. I emailed her and asked if she could help me in my quest to write a "How to Teach Phonics" booklet. I thought it would be a ten-page booklet that outlined the steps involved. She didn't know me, but graciously agreed to meet with me at a local Mexican restaurant (people in Tucson always seem to meet at Mexican restaurants when we have important work to do. Burritos and tacos seem to make the brain work better.) She has taught me so much about teaching phonological and phonemic awareness. With her guidance, my ten-page booklet grew into a two-volume Roadmap.

I also want to thank my daughter's teachers, Jill Heerboth, MS, CCC-SLP, Dr. Lynne Jaffe, Brenda Hanna M.A. Ed., and Dr. Meg Burke, for giving my daughter such loving instruction and for giving me hope when I could not see how to teach her to read and learn math.

Jill met my daughter when Janelle was just 12 months old. Jill patiently helped Janelle develop language skills that other children develop more naturally. At the time, I did not realize that language challenges and dyslexia often go hand-in-hand. I am especially grateful for Jill's hard work during the stubborn toddler years as it appears that receiving early intervention made language connections in her dyslexic brain that will last her lifetime.

Lynne taught Janelle the foundations of reading and writing while also showing me how Orton-Gillingham based programs are structured and how to adapt them to my daughter. I learned as much from her as Janelle did.

Brenda has expanded Janelle's reading and writing skills. She has been essential to the development of the DOG ON A LOG Phonics Progression. She has dedicated uncountable hours to long discussions on what steps should come next and edited my chapter and Let's GO! Books to make sure they are consistent with the needs of students.

Meg has taken the challenging language and concepts of math and made them understandable. She has also guided me in how I continue these lessons at home. I cannot imagine trying to teach math to Janelle without Meg's expertise.

Thank you to Sioux McGill for her guidance on the cover art and all her editing time. She took my covers from "meh," to adorable.

Thank you to my child editors Lily and Mahri and their mom Holly who have made sure the stories are engaging and understandable.

I want to send my thanks, appreciation, and gratitude to all the artists who have made their images available for public domain use. I photoshop these images (as well as my own photography) to create all the artwork. I can't draw, so editing these sweet images to match my stories allows me to give the readers a bit of a break from the hard job of reading. I feel like I have a community of artists helping me help kids. I especially want to thank Michael Boylan, a wildlife photographer, who has provided me with many photographs I have been thrilled to include.

And thank you to my family. My husband who has stood by me and taken the kids on solo activities so I could have a quiet house to work in. Thank you to my dear Nathan whose artistic and literary opinions are beyond his years.

And, most especially, thank you to my beloved Janelle. She is my inspiration and my most joyous editor.

With great appreciation,
Pamela Brookes

Endnotes for Hyperlinks

What if it's NOT Dyslexia

i

https://www.nationsreportcard.gov/reading_math_2015/#reading?grade=4

ii https://www.apmreports.org/story/2018/09/10/hard-words-why-american-kids-arent-being-taught-to-read

iii https://lincs.ed.gov/publications/pdf/PRFbooklet.pdf

iv

https://www.allaboutlearningpress.net/go.php?id=1605&url=4520

v https://www.explodethecode.com/

vi https://mindplay.com/

vii

https://www.highnoonbooks.com/detailHNB.tpl?eqskudatarq=FP8446-X

viii https://www.youtube.com/watch?v=J6fyNvtp1r8

ix

https://www.youtube.com/watch?v=wBuA589kfMg&fbclid=IwAR0hs62XqzvfdwTziEMJA8A5Uhs6fQ6ZGL3KljBUrTIMS1UuwAdJ-0UujTE

x http://www.allkindsofminds.org/word-decoding-blending-and-segmenting-sounds-impact-of-memory

xi

https://www.pinterest.com/search/pins/?q=phonics%20segmenting%20blending&rs=typed&term_meta%5B%5D=phonics|typed&term_meta%5B%5D=segmenting|typed&term_meta%5B%5D=blending|typed

xii https://sightwords.com/sight-words/dolch/

The Importance of Early Intervention

xiii
https://hms.harvard.edu/sites/default/files/publications%20archive/OnTheBrain/OnTheBrainFall14.pdf?fbclid=IwAR3FdX8UNRs7qh6KI_0K03zzFKaSGoc9sLbR5PM5EdBqUCI6ZGWckEkOV6U

xiv https://www.readingrockets.org/article/online-chat-dr-sally-shaywitz

xv http://dyslexia.yale.edu/the-center/our-mission/

xvi https://kidshealth.org/en/parents/dyslexia.html

xvii https://www.dyslexia.com/question/inheritance-of-dyslexia/

xviii http://dyslexiahelp.umich.edu/

xix http://dyslexiahelp.umich.edu/parents/learn-about-dyslexia/is-my-child-dyslexic/developmental-milestones/birth-6-years

xx https://www.cambridge.org/core/journals/journal-of-child-psychology-and-psychiatry-and-allied-disciplines/article/is-preschool-language-impairment-a-risk-factor-for-dyslexia-in-adolescence/793440F296AE989B6430457054D34F4E

xxi https://agesandstagesresearch.com/en

xxii

https://www.google.com/search?q=understood+org+earl y+intervention+and+what+it+is&oq=understood+org+e arly+intervention+and+what+it+is&aqs=chrome..69i57. 10423j1j7&sourceid=chrome&ie=UTF-8

xxiii https://bilingualkidspot.com/2017/10/19/benefits-importance-reading-young-children/

xxiv https://www.dys-add.com/

xxv http://www.readingrockets.org/article/phonemic-activities-preschool-or-elementary-classroom

xxvi https://homeschoolingwithdyslexia.com/teach-phonemic-awareness-kids-dyslexia/ref/70/

xxvii

https://www.pinterest.com/search/pins/?rs=ac&len=2&q =phonemic%20awareness%20activities%20preschool&e q=phonemic%20awareness&etslf=8718&term_meta%5B %5D=phonemic|autocomplete|3&term_meta%5B%5D=a wareness|autocomplete|3&term_meta%5B%5D=activitie s|autocomplete|3&term_meta%5B%5D=preschool|autoc omplete|3

xxviii https://www.smartkidswithld.org/getting-help/dyslexia/help-young-readers/

xxix https://dogonalogbooks.com/printables/

xxx

https://www.deyproject.org/uploads/1/5/5/7/15571834/r eadinginkindergarten_online-1__1_.pdf